MURIDA

Holding the Shadow of My Sister

Diya Mutasim M.D.

ISBN: 1508778604
ISBN 13: 9781508778608

CHAPTER ONE

I t was November 2007 when, on my way to Twam Cancer Hospital in the Emirates, I learned that my nieces and nephew had lied to my sister Murida. In an attempt to give their mother fresh hope, the children had told her that the oncologist would give her a stronger medication as soon as I arrived and the two of us had a chance to discuss her treatment. *It's an unfair burden*, I thought as I walked down the hallway. *But there's nothing I can do to change it.*

As soon as I opened the door to Murida's room, and before I'd walked the few steps to reach my sister's bed to hug her, she called out:

"*Khayya* Diya, where is the medicine? Did you bring it? When will I get it?"

Before I could utter a word, she added:

"Look at your sister, I can't breathe on my own, and I hate this thing." Murida pointed a finger at the oxygen outlet on the wall. "It blows air into my nose and makes it dry and painful. When will I get better? When can I go home?"

I slowly approached the hospital bed, as I had so many times in my thirty-year career as a doctor, and placed my two crutches by its side. But this was different from any of those other times. Although the room was full of people who were lined up against the walls, sitting or standing, I could see only my dear sister. I leaned against the lowered railing and waited. I could not interrupt my older sister.

"I'm sick of this place. I've been here nine days, and I'm not getting better. It's in my lungs now. I want to get better. I want to breathe without this thing." Again, she pointed to the oxygen tube. "Did you talk to the doctor?"

On this visit, Murida wasn't as welcoming of my hug as she'd been in the past. She no longer wanted me to reassure or comfort her—she wanted her brother the doctor to be the bearer of good news. She wanted me to give her a "cure for the lungs." She could take discomfort and pain, if it meant that her lungs might be cleared of cancer and she could breathe comfortably again. She was drowning in her own bed.

On that morning, I stood by my sister's side and repeated false, reassuring words: You'll be fine; yes, there's hope; I'll talk to the doctor right away. That was all I could think of to say. Somehow, I managed to stay strong. For everyone's sake, I had to behave as if Murida was an ordinary patient, not my beloved sister. I didn't want to feel very sad for her, as it would show. If I let myself experience my emotions, then my intelligent sister, who'd had such a wide variety of life experiences, would easily read those emotions on my face.

On the long journey to see her, I'd reflected on how my older sister's life had been so cruelly unfair. It wasn't unfair that she got breast cancer at age 63—that was life and its random events. But the disease could have been discovered earlier, giving Murida a better chance at survival. So many things about how her cancer was discovered and treated could've been different. I couldn't stop thinking that, even though I was thousands of miles away in the U.S., I should've helped Murida make better decisions about her health. If I had, maybe her cancer would've been discovered easily. Maybe, by November 2007, it would've been completely gone.

But things had never been easy for my hard-working sister Murida, who had fled Palestine in 1948, as a five-year-old girl. Twenty-nine years later, she was forced to leave her adopted country, Lebanon, for Dubai. It seemed that every time Murida's life settled down, a new surprise was waiting for her.

It had been a year and a half earlier, in the spring of 2006, that Murida first noticed a "boil" in her left breast the size of a ripe date. She found it one evening when she was drying herself after a bath: a hard, oval object just under the surface of the skin. At first, Murida paid it little attention. She wasn't obsessed with her health, like our hypochondriac mother and younger sister Suad. Even though Murida's nipple had been pulling inward for a few months, she thought it was a change that came with age. She thought the nodule might be an infection, a simple abscess, so she applied hot wet rags to the breast in order to bring the swelling to the surface, just as she'd learned from her mother long ago. She also took a few antibiotic pills that she'd found in her medicine chest, left over from a previous bout with the flu.

But two weeks passed, and the boil didn't shrink.

Murida didn't know much about breast health—perhaps, if she'd stayed in Beirut, she might have known more. Perhaps, if our family hadn't fled Palestine for Beirut, or if she hadn't needed to leave Beirut for Dubai, the whole course of her disease might have been different. But all of these things had happened: She'd fled Palestine to find civil war in Beirut. In the midst of the war, Murida's husband had left to work in Dubai. Six months later, when the war didn't end, Murida and her children had been compelled to join him.

But although she was pushed around by world events, my sister wasn't passive, a weak woman being tossed from one place to another.

Before the boil appeared and everything in Murida's life changed utterly, she had been firmly in control of her life. She'd always been a doer who didn't ask anyone to complete her work, solve her problems, or help her financially. No matter how hard life got, Murida Mutasim did things for herself. In 1981, she'd even passed the difficult Dubai driver's test the first time she took it, while men with significant experience driving in other countries took three or four tries to pass.

Murida had long thought of herself as a worker. She'd started her first "job" when she was just twelve, while all of us were living in the Burj al-Barajneh Palestinian refugee camp, just south of Beirut. It was the place where my family settled after fleeing Palestine in the fall of 1948, and where I was born and raised.

Yet my big sister Murida was more than just a worker. She was sharp at school. She wasn't like our oldest sister, Muhiba, who'd gotten just one year of education while still in Palestine. Muhiba had to quit school soon after starting second grade so that the family could flee the bombing of our village in northern Palestine. Not long after their arrival as refugees in Lebanon, Muhiba started work in a candy factory to help make ends meet. Meanwhile, Murida started school in Beirut and continued straight through the sixth grade. She learned how to read, write, and manage sums. It might not have been enough for university, but Murida managed to achieve great things with small resources.

After sixth grade, Murida had stayed home. Inside the family home, she became responsible for all the housework in our bustling family, which had by then grown to eight. She learned how to sew, a skill that would prove very valuable in fast-growing Dubai. Soon after their move to Dubai in November 1977, Murida bought a sewing machine and started making dresses for women in the neighborhood. Some of her earnings supplemented her husband's limited income, but the rest went into savings, which would allow her to buy her first car.

Murida hadn't sewed professionally while she lived in Lebanon, because it would've been an embarrassment not just to her, but to her whole extended family. The neighbors would've thought that Saleem was terribly poor, and Murida wasn't going to give the neighbors a reason to disrespect her family. But in Dubai, they lived among foreigners, mostly from India and Pakistan. There, Murida didn't worry as much about the family's status. Everyone around them was working class, and no one knew them very well. There, Murida felt liberated of her traditional society's expectations.

She'd been in Dubai for three years when she took a taxi to the license bureau and sailed through her driving test. The building was in the business district, where Hindi was as commonly spoken as Arabic. The woman who conducted the driving test was a short Iranian woman in her forties who, unlike Murida at the time, covered her hair. The practical part of the test involved driving on narrow roads, highways, and roundabouts. Murida did so well that the Iranian woman told her: "You're the second woman ever to pass the test on first attempt. You should be proud of yourself."

Murida had wished more people were around to hear such a great compliment. It was rare that she heard compliments from anyone.

Murida's husband Saleem spoiled the day, a little, by getting angry because he'd failed the test twice already. The men who'd tested him were mean, he kept saying. But Murida was ecstatic. Now, she could go places that sold produce in bulk instead of shopping only at the small stores near their apartment. And she wouldn't have to take taxis ever again.

For Murida, owning a car was as good as getting a university degree. Who back in the refugee camp would believe that Murida Mutasim was driving her own car, a car that she'd bought with her own money? She was proud every time someone asked the make of the car. "Mitsubishi," she would casually answer. It was a used car, yes, but a good one. What would her parents think when they learned that their second daughter was driving in the streets of Sharjah and Dubai?

Her mother would be frightened, but her father always knew that Murida was capable of anything she put her mind to, just like him.

After she had her license, Murida felt that she was the equal of those wealthy Emirati women who came to dress-making appointments at her apartment. She loved how they respected her opinions on maintaining a conservative appearance while showing off their bodies. Only a year after launching her business, she had a big following. She'd learned, by watching her refugee father, that honesty and hard work brought success.

Murida even thought that the driver's license gave her an edge over her pretty older sister Muhiba, and that she should no longer let herself feel inferior. Who else among their contemporaries had a driver's license and her own car—all while getting seven children through school and university? God worked in mysterious ways. As they said, if He closes a door, then He opens a window.

Later, however, Murida came to wish she had never driven a car. She would have preferred that God opened a different window, one that kept her illness away.

CHAPTER TWO

In the spring of 2006, Murida was home alone when my niece—her second-oldest daughter, Mona—arrived for a visit. Although Mona didn't yet know about it, the date-sized boil was weighing heavily on her mother's mind.

Murida opened the front door of her second-floor apartment to receive her daughter, who had grown into a beautiful forty-year-old woman: religious, confident, and charming. Mona hadn't always been around her mother. Five years earlier, in 2001, Mona and her children had moved to Qatar, where her husband was supervising a large construction project. To her mother's relief, Mona's family had returned to the United Arab

Emirates four years later. Now, like most of Murida's children, Mona lived in neighboring Sharjah, about a thirty-minute drive from her parents' apartment in Dubai. Even if she couldn't see her mother every day, Mona and Murida talked at least once a day on the phone.

On this hot spring day, Murida had closed the window shades to prevent the hot sun from coming in. Once Murida opened the front door, Mona noticed right away that her mother looked preoccupied. She barely reciprocated my niece's kisses on her cheeks. And, for the first time, Murida avoided looking into Mona's eyes. Usually, Murida had a big smile whenever any of her children visited—this time, there was no smile. The two walked through the dining room and into the small living room to get to their seats. Mona sipped from a coffee she'd picked up on her way, as the American coffee craze had long since reached Dubai.

"What's wrong?" Mona asked, soon after sitting down.

My sister realized that she had to open up to her dear Mona.

"I have a boil that wouldn't heal," she said, pointing to her chest. "I took twenty Ampicillin pills and it's still there."

While in Qatar, the mother of one of Mona's friends had died of breast cancer. My niece's thoughts flashed immediately to this woman, who she'd visited and prayed for so many times.

"Did you tell Dad? Or anyone else?"

"I didn't see a reason to tell your father." Murida shifted in her chair. "You know how his reaction would be an added burden. I did tell your sister Maha."

Murida thought Mona's feelings were a little hurt by this. It was a while before Mona spoke.

"What about Mahmoud?"

"I don't know what to tell him yet." Murida paused. "Do you think I might have 'the disease'?"

"God willing no."

Murida asked her daughter what she should do. Although Mona had once been her little girl, Murida had come to respect her daughter's opinions. After all, Mona had gone to university and studied journalism, and she'd mingled among people from of all walks of life.

Mona set down her coffee on a small side table that had a tissue box and an ashtray. She told her mother that she'd need a mammogram. "I've done it twice. I'll make an appointment for you with my doctor."

Mona offered to call her brother Mahmoud after making the appointment. When Murida nodded, Mona pulled out her phone and turned away before calling a doctor who was a favorite among Murida's daughters. The soonest appointment she could get with this popular doctor was three days out.

"How can I wait so long? Maha scared me a little last night, and now I need to know, soon." Murida unconsciously reached up to touch her breast. "I haven't slept the whole past week"

"It'll be okay."

"Let your brother know, but don't let him get worried. Tell him it's just a precaution."

After a two-hour chat, broken up by mother and daughter doing the noon prayers, Mona kissed her mother and stood up to leave. My niece wanted to be back in Sharjah before her children were home from school. She tried to avoid thinking about cancer. But, as she drove, her mind kept returning to it. Still, her heart, full of faith in God's goodness, didn't want to believe it.

After Mona left, Murida sat on the couch where Mona had sat, her head down, feeling stunned, worse than before Mona had come over. *The secret is out*, my sister thought, *and I can't hide from it any more.* She stared at the painting on the wall without enjoying anything in it. Mahmoud had bought it for them a year ago, and every time she looked at it, she discovered new features that pleased her: a pond, bushes with colorful flowers, a big tree, and a small far-away home by the edge of a mountain. There was no sand in a place like that, no need for daily dusting. Murida would often wish she lived in such a place, but today the painting didn't elicit any feelings.

All my sister could think about was: What if I have "the disease"?

I'll die, she thought. But no, she couldn't die yet—she had just gotten all her girls married, which she felt was her life's biggest duty. They all had children, and their husbands were educated, hard-working, and respectful. They were even respectful of Murida's husband Saleem, who never knew when to talk and when to hold his tongue. He chattered continuously, and yet they still treated him honorably. She couldn't leave Saleem, either. Who would keep an eye on him? Mahmoud would be stuck with his father, and Saleem would make his son and daughter-in-law's lives difficult.

This was supposed to be my time to enjoy myself with my kids and all their kids living close to me. Finally, the time had come when Murida no longer had to work her sewing machine to help pull in a little extra money. Their rent was cheap, and Mahmoud gave them plenty to live on.

Maybe the boil is nothing. Murida just had to put her faith in God and accept whatever He had planned for her, as her daughter Mona would say ever since she'd returned from Qatar with her head covered, a deeply religious woman. Some of us in the family—like me—had moved away from religion. But Murida still followed all His obligations. She never missed a prayer or a single day of fasting, even when she was sick. God had gotten her this far, she thought, and He would not abandon her now. She had never hurt anyone, and she'd worked so hard to bring up seven children through want, war, and emigration.

I can't die now, Murida thought. *My children still need me.* They need a mother to hold the family together—their father couldn't do that. All seven were too young to be motherless.

Murida's mind raced through all her children in order of their birth, as she did at the end of each of her five daily prayers, when she asked God to keep them well:

The first was Maha. Murida missed having her oldest daughter around. Maha was Murida's "genius." She had gotten married and moved to Abu Dhabi, where her husband worked as an accountant.

Mahmoud, Murida's second child and her only son, was a successful architect. He had three healthy boys and a good, highly educated wife. Our oldest sister Muhiba had scorned him when he was a little boy with a mild lisp, but no one could look down on him now. Murida was exceptionally proud of him.

Mona, her third, was happily married to an engineer and had two boys and a lovely, bright girl. Since Maha had left for Abu Dhabi, Mona had become her mother's other confidante.

Manal and Amal were also each married to successful engineers. Years before, Murida had thought that her daughter Amal was the least fortunate, because she was not particularly beautiful and had some of Saleem's speaking habits. But she turned out to be so lucky! Amal's husband loved her. He was rich, happy, generous, and was starting his own company. They ate meat every day, and Amal ate like a man. *God worked in special ways*, Murida thought.

Hanan, Murida's sixth, had recently immigrated to Canada with her husband. Hanan was Murida's biggest worry. The girl wasn't assertive enough and seemed to get confused easily. She "drowned in a few inches of water," as people said, and her husband was very demanding and controlling. There was also Hanan's health: She had cysts in her kidneys, which gave her bouts of severe pain until they were drained.

Finally, Murida thought of her dear, sweet youngest daughter. Since Ghina was the youngest, Murida had spent more "quality time" with her than with any of the others. So Murida well knew that her youngest was still having a hard time with her mother-in-law—her aunt Muhiba.

My oldest sister had never wanted Murida's youngest to marry her oldest son. Muhiba didn't smile once at the engagement party, and she even avoided speaking with poor Ghina. Many people noticed Muhiba's lack of enthusiasm about her son's engagement, but Murida bore it in silence. She was happy for the young couple and glad that Muhiba's son was good to her daughter. After they got married, he gave her freedom and wasn't possessive like so many men. *But,* Murida thought, *Ghina still needs me by her side.*

Seven children! Where I worked in Cincinnati, it would've seemed like a lot. But having seven children was not unusual in refugee families that had come from farming backgrounds, where many children were needed to help with the labor. But seven children would've been a lot easier to manage if my sister had found an equally strong husband.

Murida and Saleem were from similar backgrounds: Both had fled the same town in northern Palestine with their families on October 28, 1948—she as a girl of five, and he as a fifteen-year-old boy. Both of them had grown up in the same refugee camp south of Beirut, and both had elementary-school educations. Saleem was even a distant relation—the cousin of our sister Muhiba's husband.

But, despite their proximity, Murida and Saleem hadn't known each other until their engagement. All my sisters were raised so strictly that people knew of them but didn't meet them. Saleem and his brother ran a small grocery store in the camp interior, but Murida may never have seen him there, as my family shopped at a store a few steps away. Soon after her engagement, Saleem went off to work as a wallpaper hanger in Qatar. He'd planned to save a little money for the wedding and for a small home in the camp. During the few months he was away, my big sister began to think of herself as a married woman. They had done the *kitab*, which meant they were married in the eyes of God, although Murida was not to be officially wed until three years later.

When Saleem returned to Beirut, the two of them began to spend some time together at our parents' house, as was traditional for engaged couples. As they sat in the family living room with one another, Murida and my parents were surprised by Saleem's rambling way of speaking and by his sense of entitlement. He acted as though the world owed him something.

As she got to know him better, Mother was very unhappy with Saleem. She thought he was bossy and ill-mannered, and once she even threw Murida's engagement ring at him and asked him to go away. Our dad, Fayez, felt the same way, and he offered to break off the engagement. But Murida said no. She didn't think much of herself—she looked in the mirror and saw an average-looking woman in a community that prized women's beauty. It was also her turn—she was already the age at which Muhiba had been married. Most importantly, marriage to Saleem was her fate. If she canceled the engagement, her value as a bride would decrease. At least this way, she'd get her own place, where she would no longer take orders from our mother. Ever since Muhiba had left the house, Mother had asked Murida to help more and more.

Murida must have felt, in looking at her older sister Muhiba's sweet, attractive husband, that she had gotten the lesser of the two cousins. Muhiba's husband was charming, well-spoken, and wrote poetry for his young wife and children. Yet my bad-luck sister swallowed down any bitterness she felt.

So Murida married Saleem in the summer of 1961, and together they had seven children. It was sixteen years later, November 1977, at one of the peaks of Lebanon's long civil war, when all nine of them had to leave for Dubai and start a new life. I was still at home, relatively safe, in my fourth year of medical school at the American University in Beirut hospital. I was fortunate that the AUB was Beirut's West side. As Palestinians (whether Muslim or Christian), we couldn't risk trips to Christian East Beirut, which was where Saleem worked. He would definitely have been killed.

When Murida and Saleem had first gotten married, they'd lived in a one-bedroom shack that replaced the store he'd run in the Burj el-Barajneh refugee camp. For years, people had been building in the camp so haphazardly that there were hardly any decent spots left. Their house was far from our parents, and so close to the neighbors that they had no privacy.

Murida and Saleem were sandwiched between a nasty man who seemed to take a sexual interest in his own daughter in a room on the second floor, and a woman who was always screaming at her children, even at night. Later, when Murida and Saleem's children began filling the house, he added another small room to the side and one on top.

But, through it all, Murida was patient. After all, she saw that Muhiba's home was no bigger than her own. Murida only wished she lived closer to our family, so that we could spend more time together. It didn't help that Murida visited rarely, both because of the distance and because she feared being embarrassed by Saleem's behavior.

By 1977, my family had left the camp to live in an apartment in the newly erected Mutasim Building, which was in a quieter neighborhood outside the camp. But Murida and Saleem left Beirut before they could move. When the Lebanese civil war prevented Saleem from getting to work in Christian East Beirut, he went off to work in the Emirates, where his sister had already moved along with her daughters. It wasn't long before the rest of the family followed.

The memory of the day they left was seared in my mind as well as Murida's. She felt terrible for leaving all of us, and even though I was a medical student in my early twenties, I could not stop sobbing as I held tight to my older sister, just as I had nine years earlier when my sister Inaam had gotten married and moved to Jordan. Still, as much as Murida might have wished it otherwise, she couldn't stay in Beirut while Saleem worked in Dubai. He needed Murida, and she needed him. After 1948, it was the fate of Palestinians to be always on the move, going to countries that provided them opportunities for work. It would soon be my fate as well.

All in all, this move wasn't bad. But Murida missed her parents and brothers and sisters terribly, and we missed her. Tickets were expensive, and it was six years before she could go back. Meanwhile, our oldest sister Muhiba was able to bring up her children almost next door to their grandparents and three uncles. Muhiba even took over our parents' large home on the outer edge of the camp when we left in June 1974.

CHAPTER THREE

.

Breast cancer never really left Mona's mind as she drove back to Sharjah that spring day in 2006. Mona loved her mother fiercely, and Murida occupied a huge space in Mona's life: She was Mona's friend and confidante, her cheerleader, her untiring source of moral support. Mona had always enjoyed her mother's unconditional approval. But—Mona thought with a twinge—if their mother were sick, it would be even harder on Mahmoud. He was an only son who was very attached and committed to his parents. How could she possibly tell her brother?

Mahmoud loved his parents. On religious holidays, he still offered to kiss Murida's hand, just like a little boy, in appreciation for all she'd done for him. Murida had given him the best of her love, which she managed to do without spoiling him. Murida had learned from her experiences with our brother Mutasim, who was spoiled by our family, as so many first-born sons were. Mutasim felt such entitlement that he abused his sisters, both older and younger, hitting and biting them until they got married and left home.

Murida had favored Mahmoud, nursing him the longest of all her children, and even as a boy he was the other "man of the house." But, unlike our brother, Mahmoud showered his sisters with love and support. The sisters might disagree with one another, but no one disagreed with Mahmoud.

Finally, when she was home staring at the empty blue sky through her kitchen window on the fortieth floor, Mona pulled out the phone and dialed my nephew, who was still at his office.

After traditional greetings were exchanged, Mona found it difficult to unburden her mind.

"By the way I was at mother's…." Mona struggled to get the words out. "She has a thing in her breast, so I got her an appointment with the Indian doctor."

"What?"

"It's probably nothing, but I made an appointment for her to see Dr. Sandhir. You know her." Mona tried to sound calm. "Hopefully it's nothing. But we have to make sure it is not cancer."

"But she's so careful!" Mahmoud got up from the desk in his Dubai office and paced toward the window. Beyond it was the clear spring sky and Emirati skyscrapers. "She does yearly screening tests. Wouldn't they have shown something?"

"She does blood tests. She's never had a mammogram."

"Should she have?"

"Maybe"

"Why didn't Uncle Diya ever ask her to do one? He's a doctor, and she always told him the results of her yearly tests."

Later, when they told me about these conversations, I would wince. Should I have told her to have a mammogram? Was it my responsibility? I would wrestle with this question for a long time.

"I don't know," Mona said, wishing that she'd told her mother to do it. Mona had already had two mammograms while in her late thirties. Mona felt a flash of guilt, but put her trust in God.

"Should I call her now?" Mahmoud asked.

"Wait until tomorrow. She might get more worried if we make a big deal out of it. You know how much she worries."

It wouldn't have been easy to talk about getting a mammogram. Murida, like many Palestinian women of her generation, didn't feel that cancer was like other diseases. Cancer was a living creature that created its own space inside a person's body and took it over. Cancer was *evil*. That was why people didn't test for it or even use its name—for fear that they might invite it in.

Instead, people referred to it as "the disease," "that disease," "the nameless," or "the disease that we may never have to face." Even many doctors didn't use the word *cancer*. Instead, they told patients that they had "chronic inflammation," which the intuitive patient and their relatives understood to mean "the disease." When our nephew Waleed—Muhiba's second son—developed colon cancer in 1985, he wasn't told the truth about his disease, even after he admitted to his mother that he knew what he had. It was popularly believed that knowledge of the disease might rid the patient of the will to live.

A few years after Murida left Lebanon, she heard that one of our neighbors in the Burj al-Barajneh camp had developed breast cancer. I was still in Lebanon at the time, and saw this woman when she visited relatives who lived in our building. This woman, unlike others, famously talked about her condition. Everyone in the camp knew about the woman who lost her hair—and a breast—to the disease. Twenty years later, in 2006, the woman was still alive. Not just alive, but she was still happily married, even though she had only one breast. It was a story that would frequently re-enter Murida's mind as she prepared to see a doctor about the strange lump in her breast.

When Murida went in for her first doctor visit, it was another ordinary Dubai spring day. The air was blisteringly hot, and there were no clouds to shield the earth from the sun's heat and ultraviolet rays.

The night before, Murida had taken a long bath, as she usually did before a doctor visit. That night had been harder than the previous nights. She must have awakened a dozen times, as her mind wandered between hope and anguish. She considered giving up the doctor visit and putting her fate in God's hands. But no, she couldn't. For her children's sake, for Saleem's sake, and for herself, she had to go. She had been in charge all her life and she couldn't give that up now.

Stop being pessimistic, Murida told herself. *You might just have an infection that needs a stronger antibiotic. Please, God, be kind to me.* Murida promised to obey God's principles even more fiercely, to pray more often, to fast on days beyond Ramadan, to go to Mecca another time, and never to speak or hear ill of anyone. She would say *I declare that there is no god but Allah and that Mohammad is his prophet* every time she wanted her thoughts to stop their frightening paths.

On this morning, just as on other mornings, Murida got dressed and ready, although she wasn't quite honest with Saleem about where she was going: She said she was going to the "female doctor" for her yearly exam. Mahmoud had left his house in the hazy early morning and parked at a nearby Starbucks, and Mona picked up her brother at the coffee shop so that they wouldn't have to explain themselves to Mahmoud's wife. For the time being, my sister wanted her condition kept private.

As they planned it, by the time Mona and Mahmoud arrived, Saleem had already left for his daily adventures, perambulating around the neighborhood, visiting friends in stores and coffee shops. Although Murida was expecting them, when she opened the door for her two children, her legs felt suddenly weak. She knew that the time for truth had come—it couldn't be delayed any longer.

After a moment's fumbling, Murida went back into the apartment to get her purse. At Mona's suggestion, she also took a full pill of anxiety medication. The half-tablet of Xanax that Murida occasionally took when she felt too anxious would not be enough for today.

As they walked down the stairs to the car, Murida and her two children exchanged their usual greetings, but they were surrounded by an unusual tension, a new force that put a distance between them for the first time. Mahmoud didn't kiss his mother, and she was oddly relieved. For some reason, on that morning, she didn't want his display of affection. There was only worry and preparations for the worst on her mind.

As Mona drove from their public-housing complex through neighborhoods with small shops and stores to wide streets with stop lights and high residential buildings, Murida didn't feel the passing of time. She wanted time to stop. She didn't want to see the doctor. If she didn't see the doctor, then maybe—just maybe—none of it would be true.

As the car moved through the city, Murida could see the skyscrapers slide by. Dubai had changed so much in past three decades, and so had her life. *Why can't time go backwards?* Murida had recently seen an American movie where people went back in time and changed the present—why couldn't it be true? *They've invented so many miraculous things, so why can't they do this? Fifty years ago, people went to the moon. If I went back in time, I could do a mammogram and they would discover "it," but it would be the size of a pea. It would be small and easily curable.*

Although the city had changed a great deal, health care had not kept pace with other developments. Murida wondered why her "female" doctor hadn't asked her to do a breast x-ray. She also naturally wondered why I hadn't suggested it.

Why didn't they suggest it on Emirati TV? They talked about so many health and nutrition issues on Emirati television, Murida thought, but they never discussed breast cancer. She imagined that the religious censors wouldn't allow it. But who cared which food has which vitamin if they couldn't discuss something as important as breast cancer?

Finally, the three of them arrived. The clinic was in a busy business district, on the ground floor of a two-story building. In the adjacent plaza, there was a tiny storefront restaurant that sold whole roast chicken. Like most people she knew, Murida loved roast chicken with garlic-flavored mayonnaise dressing. But on that morning, the restaurant's strong, greasy smell made her nauseous. If she was spared from having the disease, then she vowed to God that she would give up roast chicken.

Inside, they registered with the woman behind the glass, who was Pakistani but spoke some Arabic. There were only ten seats: Murida, Mona, and Mahmoud were fortunate to have three together for the long wait. Across from them, a young Indian man coughed continuously. Before they entered, they'd seen him smoking outside. To their right, an Emirati woman sat covered in black except for her face. She had a restless little boy with her who wouldn't stay still. The woman kept whispering for him to stop, but the boy never did.

Except for the little boy, the waiting area was eerily quiet. The carpet was stained with coffee, and the chairs were old. After what seemed like a terribly long time, Murida's name was finally called. The three of them stood up and went in. At least, Murida thought, the wait was over. Whatever happened from now on would be irreversible. The truth, good or bad, would reveal itself.

CHAPTER FOUR

Murida's doctor was a 40-something Indian woman, tall and pretty. She was dressed in Western clothing, but had the traditional red dot between her eyebrows. She smiled as she greeted Murida, Mona, and Mahmoud in her imperfect Arabic.

On the doctor's desk, she had photographs of two young girls. Mona settled into a chair and reminded Dr. Sandhir that she and her sisters were regular patients.

"How are Amal and Manal?" Dr. Sandhir asked.

"Very well, thank you. They really like and respect you."

There were only two chairs, so Mahmoud stood by the wall to his mother's right. Mona sat to her left.

"So," the doctor said. "What brings you here today, madam?"

As they'd agreed on the way to the doctor, Mona explained what had happened, how her mother had discovered the "abscess" in her left breast, how she had taken antibiotics, and how it still hadn't gone away.

"How long have you known about the swelling?"

"I noticed it six weeks ago, as I was drying myself and looking in the mirror," Murida said. "It didn't hurt."

"Have you noticed anything else with either breast?"

"Yes. My left nipple has been pulling in—"

Dr. Sandhir interrupted. "For how long?"

"For about six months, but it doesn't hurt either"

The doctor nodded. "Is there breast cancer in your family?"

Murida felt herself tremble a little. She wondered why the doctor had jumped so quickly to cancer, saying the word with so little hesitation.

"No," Mona answered.

"Okay," the doctor said. "Do you have any chronic illnesses for which you take medication on a regular basis?"

"No. Nothing I'm very healthy."

"Okay, then. Let's go to the examination room. Sir, please stay here. Miss, you can come if you like."

As they walked to the examination room, my sister wondered why the doctor had asked about a history of breast cancer and chronic illnesses. Perhaps it was good, since the answer to both questions was a definite *no*.

Inside the exam room, Murida knew she would have to take off her blouse. It made her uncomfortable, and she turned away from the doctor and her daughter as she unbuttoned. All her life, Murida had been very private.

In the early days in the refugee camp, when Murida was a girl and before I was born, they'd had to use public bathrooms. Everything was close together at the camp, and people said that a few aggressive young men had hung close to the girls' bathrooms, trying to get a glimpse of something. Even as a child, Murida was so self-conscious that she developed a nervous bladder and constipation.

Once Murida was settled, she placed the sheet over her all the way up to her neck, just like the way she liked to be covered when sleeping in bed. The doctor, who was on the right side of the exam table, uncovered her right breast. By the time the doctor's hand reached the right breast to examine it, Murida lifted her head a little. "This one's fine. It's the left one."

"I remember. But I need to check your normal breast first in order to judge the other one. Women differ in the type of tissue in their breasts. What's normal for one may be abnormal for another."

Murida looked surprised, so the doctor went on: "It depends on many things—the woman's age, whether she's still menstruating, and the number of children she's had."

At this point, my sister's heart leapt. *Could the swelling in my left breast be normal for me? Ya Rab, Oh my God. That would be a miracle.*

The doctor palpated the right breast with both hands squeezing and kneading it. Murida wondered why her "female doctor" never did that—she just laid her one hand over it and said everything was fine. Then Dr. Sandhir covered the right breast and exposed the left one. Murida's heart was racing, her mind now numb.

The doctor first inspected the left breast visually, as if eying a melon before tapping it for quality. Murida could tell the doctor was looking straight at the lump and the indentation that had pulled in her nipple. The doctor started feeling the normal part of the breast first before moving to the lump. At first, she went over it gently. Then she held the lump between two fingers to feel its consistency. It hurt a little.

Although questions flashed through Murida's mind, she didn't interrupt the doctor: That would be bad manners. She could wait until the examination was finished. The doctor's hand moved under Murida's armpit and pushed down more firmly than she had on the breast.

Murida shifted slightly from the discomfort. *Why is she feeling there?*

After that, the doctor pulled the sheet over Murida's breasts and moved her hands over Murida's abdomen before listening to her heart and lungs.

Mona was watching the doctor's face and wondered: *What happened to the smile on the doctor's face? Her lips have tightened and her forehead became furrowed. She suddenly looked concerned.*

In the other room, Mahmoud was waiting by the wall. For the whole time his mother was being examined, he did not sit down. After all, he was a man and had to be strong. As he waited, he didn't know what to think, what to wish for. Did it even matter? Everything was in God's hands now.

Mahmoud had a deep faith, as strong as Maha's and Mona's. They had all been influenced by the heavy religion teaching in Dubai's public schools. Religion said that Mahmoud would have to accept whatever came next—it would be God's will. Still, he hoped that his mother didn't have cancer. *Help her God. You are capable of everything. She sacrificed so much so that we have a good life.*

The doctor stepped back into her office and settled down behind her desk. Immediately, Mahmoud asked about his mother's condition.

"We'll all talk together," the doctor said. "They're coming."

Soon, Murida and Mona entered and sat in the same places as before. As Mahmoud said later, it seemed that the look on Dr. Sandhir's face had changed. Her smile had been replaced by a look of concern.

Murida leaned on her daughter to make the few steps back into the doctor's office—even her legs were failing her. As Murida sat back down in her chair, she tried hard to control her shaking. A cold sweat had broken out all over her, and her heart was racing. Although the examination room was very cold, her armpits were stuck to her polyester blouse from all the nervous sweat. She knew that whatever the doctor said might change her life dramatically, more than any words that had come before. This may be the most difficult anticipation of news she ever experiences, harder than anticipating the baby's gender uttered by the midwife. She could barely breathe. Even though she inhaled as deeply as she could, it felt as though the oxygen wasn't reaching her lungs. She remembered that I had experienced the same problem when I was a young teenager, and the doctor had diagnosed it as "nerves." The doctor shuffled a few papers, and Murida looked away. The look on the doctor's face said it all. Murida wanted to leave.

"You know I'm not a cancer doctor. I'm a generalist, but I know a lot about breast diseases, as most of my patients are women. I can't say for sure what your mother has."

Murida shivered.

"It is possible that it's cancer. We have to do a mammogram, and most likely a biopsy."

Dr. Sandhir promised to get Murida in for a mammogram as soon as possible. The doctor, who had been practicing in the UAE for eleven years, knew that Murida would also need a biopsy; later, we discovered she was certain Murida had cancer. But Dr. Sandhir had learned that, in the UAE, she shouldn't give bad news right away.

Murida was right to say that there was no history of breast cancer in the family. But that didn't mean family members hadn't succumbed to other types of cancer.

It was the spring of 1985 when our oldest sister, Muhiba, frantically called me while I was working on medical research in Baltimore. It was 4 a.m. when the phone rang, and my roommate woke me up. The usually strong and controlled Muhiba could hardly organize her words. "Waleed has cancer," she said, all in a jumble. "Call Dr. Ghaleb Saab. He said you know him."

Her son Waleed, who was then just nineteen, had developed a lump in his neck and had gone to the infirmary at the American University in Beirut (AUB), where he was studying engineering. A biopsy revealed cancer, possibly from the abdomen. Muhiba had first called her husband, who flew home from Dubai where he had been working for three years, and Waleed had an exploratory laparotomy. The cancer turned out to be in his colon.

By the time they discovered it, the cancer had already spread to the connective tissue surrounding his intestines, his lymph nodes, and his liver. It was not possible to operate. The oncologist, a short, low-key, and gentle man who I knew well, took my sister and brother-in-law into a conference room and gave them the news as Waleed was recovering from the laparotomy.

The whole extended family was devastated by gentle young Waleed's terminal diagnosis. Waleed had just entered the AUB's school of engineering, and he was prized by everyone in the family. He was smart, religious, respectful, funny, and a good listener. Muhiba never stopped thinking that someone close to her must have given Waleed the evil eye, just as my mother blamed my polio on the evil eyes of the old woman next door.

CHAPTER FIVE

On the way back home from the appointment with Dr. Sandhir, none of the three said a word. This time, Mahmoud drove, and Mona sat with her mother in the back. Mona wanted to support her mother, but she couldn't find the strength or the knowhow. She couldn't even hold her mother's hand to give her some small comfort.

Although my niece was strong, Mona had never been in a position to support her mother emotionally. Only Maha—the eldest—had ever done that, but never in such a complicated situation. It was usually Murida who comforted everyone else.

They arrived at Murida's apartment, and Mona and Mahmoud went upstairs with their mother. They didn't know what to say, but they couldn't leave her alone. As they climbed the stairs, Murida looked dazed and didn't speak. She seemed to take short pauses between some steps as if she were thinking about something important or didn't want to go home. Outside the apartment, she handed her keys to her son so that he could open the door.

Inside, they went through the dining room into the adjacent living room. Mona stood waiting as her mother used the bathroom. It was only after Murida took a seat that Mona sat down in the chair to her mother's left.

"We should tell Father," Mona said. "He's going to wonder what's going on when he sees you like this."

Murida shrugged. "Whatever you like. One of you can tell him, but not here. Take him out and talk to him. I can't handle how he might react."

"Okay," Mahmoud said. "He should be coming any minute now. I'll go down, take him to the Pakistani restaurant, and tell him there."

"What will you tell him?" Mona asked.

"That Mother has a lump, and it will be tested soon."

Murida nodded.

"I'll take your car," Mahmoud said. "You're staying, right?"

Mahmoud looked at his sister, briefly, before he went downstairs to stand by Mona's car, waiting for his father to arrive. It wasn't long before his father strolled up.

Mahmoud walked toward his father, who asked why he was standing there.

"I came to take you to the Pakistani restaurant that you like."

Saleem looked surprised. "You left work to take me to a restaurant? Why?"

"I also want to talk about something."

"It's your mother, isn't it?"

Mahmoud opened the car door. "I'll tell you on the way. Let's go now."

Saleem agreed, but he slid into the front passenger seat looking confused. "So what's wrong with your mother? I'm not stupid, you know. I noticed that she hasn't been herself the last few days."

Mahmoud backed out, his tires crunching as he drove toward the main street. Although the streets in Murida's neighborhood were asphalted, the asphalt was covered over with desert sand. "We just got back from the doctor's office, and Mother has a lump in her breast. She'll have an x-ray test the day after tomorrow, and most likely the doctors will also need to test the lump."

"So what is it?"

"We don't know yet."

Saleem paused for a while. "It's not *the disease*, right?
"God willing it's not."

They soon came to the Pakistani restaurant, but Saleem didn't want to stop. "I don't want to go there. Just get me two chicken shawarma sandwiches, and I'll eat them in the car."

"All right, and I'll get three more sandwiches for me, Mona, and Mother. After that, we'll go straight back home."

Saleem agreed, and Mahmoud kept driving to the Lebanese carry-out place that sold shawarma as good as any in Beirut. Mahmoud ordered the sandwiches and called his sister, who was eager to know how her father had reacted to the news.

Back in the apartment, Mona made tea for her mother and Arabic coffee for herself, a habit she'd picked up in Qatar. For the whole time Mahmoud was gone, Murida barely spoke, and Mona rested in the adjacent bedroom. She was exhausted by the day's experience and the sleeplessness of the previous night.

It wasn't long before Mahmoud and Saleem arrived with sandwiches. Saleem, unlike his wife, was not at a loss for words. "Why didn't you tell me?"

Mona heard the noise and woke up. As he sat down, Saleem continued "You'll be fine. God is great, and He will protect you against all ills."

Mahmoud echoed with "*inshaallah*, God willing," but Murida remained silent.

Murida could not finish the small sandwich; her mouth was too dry. After more silence, Saleem turned on the TV. He listened to the mid-afternoon *adhan*, which announced the call for prayer. Saleem gazed at the TV for a few moments before he got up to wash and pray in the adjacent room.

When Saleem was gone, Murida spoke. "Mona, you need to go make dinner. Your husband and children will be getting home soon."

Mona assured her mother that she could stay, and that Mahmoud would go to his office and then pick her up at the end of the day. Mahmoud wasn't sure about leaving his mother in this state, but she asked him to go.

At the word "cancer," all sorts of thoughts rushed into Murida's head. She hadn't been living in Beirut when our nephew Waleed was diagnosed, but she knew that Muhiba was devastated by the news. She herself had been shocked to learn that her sweetest and smartest nephew had cancer. *God protect Mahmoud* was the first thing she uttered after learning the news.

Waleed's parents continued to hold onto a sense that he just might make it, even though the oncologist told them he had only about three months to live. They kept hiding their feelings and doing their best to present him with a positive front. After a short visit, Waleed's father had gone back to Dubai to earn money for his wife and five children. As a PLO sympathizer, it wasn't safe for him in Lebanon during that phase of the civil war.

But Muhiba's husband wasn't a fighter: He was a gentle man. He read more than most men of his generation—about politics, history, and literature. He wrote poetry and loved his wife deeply. He valued her discipline and thriftiness, how she was raising and educating six children on a small income. Indeed, he'd gone into a happy shock when my father had agreed to his marriage to Muhiba—after all, he was such a "small" man, with no degree or lucrative career, just a simple hotel doorman. Muhiba, meanwhile, was a beautiful and commanding woman, unlike my hard-working sister Murida.

Around seven p.m., as the sun set and darkness fell on the desert, cooling the air, Mahmoud returned for Mona. The two of them drove back to Sharjah together, where they lived only a few minutes apart. When they left, Saleem was blithely watching TV in the living room. Either he was in denial, they thought, or he couldn't comprehend the potential seriousness of his wife's condition.

After her two children left, Murida changed into a nightgown and went to her bedroom. She passed by the second bedroom, where her girls had once slept on make-shift mattresses on the floor. There was also a bed that, during the day, had doubled as a place for the children to spread out their homework and study. In Murida's home, studying had always come first, a rule she shared with our mother and many Palestinian refugee families.

Now, as she sat down on her bed, Murida's brain was numb, and she was unable to focus. She couldn't think clearly, but in a way that was a relief. She wished she could switch off her brain and float in the absent bliss she'd first experienced when she mistakenly took a double dose of her anxiety medication years ago.

She wasn't even sure what she was feeling. Maybe it was a new emotion, or maybe it was such a jumble that it would be impossible to name the individual emotions, just as when liquids are mixed together and the individual ingredients can no longer be identified.

Finally, Murida fell asleep, but she woke every hour or two. She was relieved when she heard the early morning *adhan* from the neighboring mosque, signaling an end to the darkness. She'd loved the soothing sound of the *adhan* since her early days in the refugee camp, even though it also meant she had to wake up and help her mother make dough to take to the local oven. But on this early morning, it had an additional liberating effect. She got up and performed her prayers, and a few extras, for which she would get "extra credit," as the scholars said.

Then, instead of going back to sleep, Murida went into the kitchen and made a pot of sweet tea. Among all the things around her, it was the only one that still made sense. She'd drunk tea with breakfast since she was a child. She couldn't see herself cooking, although she knew that she'd feel compelled to—it was her duty. Throughout her illness, even when suffering great distress, Murida would continue to do her duties. That's how my sister was.

Murida had always been particularly joyful in doing her duty by her son Mahmoud, who she'd felt from the beginning was special. She'd nursed him for two full years, longer than any of his sisters. She loved him feeding on her, falling asleep on her chest. She hated putting him to sleep away from her and wanted him to be by her side all the time, even though it wasn't possible—she had to take care of Maha, the house, and Saleem.

From a young age, Mahmoud had been the other man of the house, and he was up for it. He was good at solving his sisters' problems, both personal and academic, and they all looked up to him, just as Murida had taught them. He was logical and commonsensical like his mother and grandfather—Murida thanked God that he resembled our side of the family. Mahmoud turned out like her brothers: smart at school and successful in his work. Although he was a small boy with a lisp, she always knew he could do anything.

It ate at her when, during their days in the refugee camp, Mahmoud would come home from Auntie
Muhiba's house, saying that his aunt wouldn't let him
inside. He could see through the window that his cousin Khaled was in there, but Aunt Muhiba had refused
to open the door, claiming Khaled was not around to
play. It broke Murida's heart, but she never complained
to our older sister or to our parents.

CHAPTER SIX

It seemed to take forever for the morning of the mammogram to arrive.

As in all the nights that week, Murida slept little, with many interruptions from nightmares and bad thoughts. She wanted the morning to come—for the night to be over, the wait to be over. She was now on an irreversible path, and she couldn't stop for anything. She'd made up her mind. Whatever the outcome of the tests, she needed to know the truth. After this, she wouldn't live in the unknown, as she had for the last few weeks. She wouldn't be like her nephew Waleed, who was never told his diagnosis. She believed in the saying: "He who fears death dies every day, but he who doesn't dies only once." And yet she wanted to live, not die!

Again, it was Mona who came to take her mother to the hospital. Mona, too, had barely slept the night before. Her husband was surprised by her jittery, anxious mood, and she was no longer able to keep her mother's condition a secret. Mona found herself confessing the whole thing, and found relief in sharing her worries with someone close. Finally, she was able to cry.

Murida felt that God had been good to daughter Mona, and Mona deserved it. Mona's husband was a good man—an engineer from the AUB who'd also come from a struggling Palestinian family. His family was from the same town as theirs, which was a source of pride: good girls married men from their parents' towns. Less fortunate girls married men whose families were from other Palestinian towns. If they were very unfortunate, they might even marry non-Palestinians.

Mona had been pretty from birth and good in school. It was true that Mona was not as intelligent as Maha and Mahmoud, but those two were unrealistically smart, perhaps geniuses. None of Murida's other children would be able to match the eldest two in intelligence.

But Mona had other gifts. She was well-behaved, obedient, helpful in housework, and good spirited. She was also liked by her teachers, who looked to her to be a role model for the other girls in her class.

Mona was twelve when the family left Beirut. She continued to be good at school and, like Maha and Mahmoud, got a scholarship to study at al-Ain University, two hours away. Gradually, as the years passed, she became her mother's second confidante, after Maha. When Mona's husband got a new job, and Mona left with him for Qatar in 2001, Murida sank into a long depression. Maha was already two hours away in Abu Dhabi, and now Mona was leaving as well.

Murida needed at least one of the two to be nearby. Dear Mahmoud was not the same as having one of her oldest daughters. When Mona and her family returned to the UAE four years later, Murida was elated, and the two became closer than ever. But, in the spring of 2006, that close relationship would be challenged.

Mona parked easily in front of the hospital, as there were many open spots. She and Murida stayed close together as they stepped through the automatic glass door and then stopped. They looked around, confused, before a man in a hospital uniform called out to them. He offered to help, and Mona asked for the mammogram area.

The man pointed to green lines on the floor and gave them detailed instructions on how to reach radiology. Once they were upstairs, Mona registered and paid a young man behind glass for the test. The two of them were taken directly back to mammography.

A hesitant-seeming young technician greeted them. She explained the procedure to both of them before she asked Mona to return to the waiting room. After her daughter left, Murida slowly removed her blouse and bra.

In those moments, my sister focused so intently on the machine that she felt it was alive and even had a moral sense. Murida hoped that the machine would be kind to her and not detect cancer. Her fate was in the hands of this thing: If the machine was kind, then she would be saved. They said that God worked His ways through anything He chooses, so He could choose this machine to direct Murida's destiny.

The procedure took longer than she expected. It may have taken twenty minutes—Murida wasn't sure. It was startling and uncomfortable, with the technician kneading her breast and pushing it and squeezing it into the proper space in the machine. The technician also seemed to look taken back as she felt for the knot. Finally, the technician told Murida she was finished.

Murida was hesitant. "So—what is it? What do you see?"

"I don't know. I'm just a technician. The doctor has to read the test."

"How long will that take?"

The technician shook her head. "The doctor isn't here. He'll read the test, someone will type the report, the doctor signs it, and then your doctor will get the report and she'll tell you the result."

"When?"

"I'm sorry, but you have to ask your doctor."

Murida shook her head. She needed to know more.

"Give it two or three days. Actually, tomorrow is the weekend, and the radiology doctors are off. So give it four."

Murida turned away from the technician, who was finishing up her work. My usually patient sister seethed with frustration. *Doesn't the doctor understand how patients feel while waiting for the result of important tests? This is a matter of life and death! Don't they have mothers and sisters?* Murida would've understood the delay if she'd gone to a public hospital, as she'd offered, but Mahmoud and Mona had insisted she come to a private one.

The technician asked Murida to get dressed and left the room. Murida stood in the room for a while, crying quietly, feeling helpless and hungry for air.

Murida had felt this kind of overwhelming helplessness a few times before. The feeling had come most powerfully when she'd looked at her newborns and realized that she was having girl after girl. After her second-born was a boy, she'd felt hopeful that she would have one or two more boys. Yet five consecutive deliveries had resulted in five girls. What had she done to deserve six girls and only one boy? Our mother had three boys and our older sister Muhiba had three of each.

Murida spent years wishing for another boy. She was pregnant with a boy one more time, but miscarried. It had been a terrible day. Maha had come to ask her grandmother to go check on Murida, who had severe cramps. They'd already called for the midwife. By the time our mother arrived, Murida was crying out in pain while lying on her side and pulling her knees to up to her chest. Her four children were crying in silence in the next room. She was devastated when her mother showed her the tiny dead boy's penis.

The worst period of sadness came right after Murida had delivered Amal, when depression hit her like a storm. Murida didn't want to look at her own newborn and she hated nursing the baby. *Who hates her own baby?* Murida had wondered, feeling guilty.

When the midwife came back two days after the birth to check on my sister, she was shocked at Murida's state. She said that she'd seen cases like this, but Murida's was the worst. Murida could barely motivate herself to cook, and she had no one to help her. Maha was eight and offered to help, God bless her. But she was already in third grade and had to study.

The post-partum depression came back a year later, with Hanan, although it wasn't as bad. But ever since that time these feelings of anxiety and doom never completely left Murida, just as they'd never completely left me between the ages of ten and twenty-two.

Mona came in just as Murida finished getting dressed. The technician had told Mona that the test was over, and that it would be as many as four days before the report was sent to the doctor. Mona hurried into the room, knowing how upset her mother must feel.

"How was it?"

Murida shrugged. "There was a little pain, but we won't know the result for four days. I saw the pictures on the TV screen, they're done. Someone has to check them that's all."

Mona nodded.

"They have no heart. For them, it's just a business. They took their money already, so they don't care. No one feels the pain of the one who's waiting."

On their way to the car, Mona suggested they go out to a Lebanese restaurant for tea and zaatar pies. She didn't want her mother to go home just yet. "It's between meals, so the place will be almost empty. You must be hungry since you haven't had breakfast."

Murida agreed. "Did you call Mahmoud?"

"We'll call him while we're at the restaurant."

"All right. My brain is so numb I'm not sure I can make a meal today without burning it."

"Don't worry about cooking." Mona stretched out a hand toward her mother. "We can get roast chicken or shawarma or biryani carryout. Dad loves 'outside food,' he'll be happy with anything made in a restaurant."

Murida preferred home-cooked food for many reasons. For a few years after she'd had her last baby—her daughter Ghina—Murida was overweight. She soon learned that it wasn't healthy to be overweight, and particularly that it wasn't good for your blood pressure. After that, she went on a strict diet and lost thirty pounds, returning to the weight she'd been in her mid-twenties.

My brother-in-law Saleem, on the other hand, loved to eat and ate as much food as was in front of him. Thin in his youth, he progressively gained weight until he almost doubled his size by the time he was seventy. Although his children urged him to lose weight and eat healthier, he continued to eat as he wanted, even after he was diagnosed with heart disease.

Once, I was surprised at Saleem's weight gain and asked Murida, "What do you feed him?" Although I was trying to be funny, Murida was hurt. It took her two days before she confessed how upset I'd made her.

"He is not an animal to feed."

I apologized.

This was not the first time Murida's pride was injured by real or perceived insults to Saleem. Our brother Mutasim would, along with Muhiba's husband, pick on Saleem in public and mock him. It made Murida angry and deeply hurt to see her husband defenseless or clueless. The insults seemed to slide right off him, but she fought back against whoever was mocking Saleem. For her children's sake, she could not allow it. No matter what, Saleem had to be shown respect.

As Mona had suggested, the Cedars restaurant was nearly empty. The morning crowd was gone, and its large open space was filled with empty tables that were covered with plastic-lined sheets. Mona and Murida sat at a table in a corner and ordered tea along with cheese and zaatar pies. Murida loved flatbread pies with anything on them, especially melted cheese. But after the mammogram, she could take only a few small bites. Her mouth was so dry that she had to take a sip of tea with each bite, and it was hard to swallow.

Mona looked over at her mother's plate. "You're not eating much."

"I don't have an appetite."

"…"

"I wish I didn't have to go home." Murida's forehead wrinkled.

"Why?"

"Your father doesn't understand how I feel. He expects me to behave normally, and I can't be touched right now. Last night, he got upset with me. The only one he loves is himself." Murida paused and sipped her tea.

Mona gave her mother an understanding smile.

"He's not a mean man; he just can't put himself in anyone else's shoes. It's all about him—as if he never grew up."

"I know."

"Your brother thinks the fact that Saleem was abandoned by his mother is a reason to behave the way he does." Murida paused. "I just wish your father could go to Mahmoud's house for a few days. I don't have energy for his moodiness and his needs, not until I get the test results."

They were sitting at the table, Murida still poking at her food, when Mona called Mahmoud. He was disappointed to hear that it would be so long before they knew anything. Mahmoud knew his mother well, and he was sure that she would be impatient.

Mahmoud asked Mona if he could talk to his mother, but when Mona pulled the phone away from her ear, Murida shook her head. Quietly, Murida asked Mona to tell her brother that she couldn't talk just now. Suddenly, Murida had tears in her eyes. Her head was turned away, but Mona saw her mother's chin quivering and her lips shut tight. This was the first time she had not welcomed a call from her son, or anyone else for that matter.

Mona wasn't sure what to do, but she respected her mother's wishes.

Mona had always loved her mother. Over the years, Mona grew to admire her mother as well, and to see her as a fellow human being who needed emotional and moral support. It took Mona a long time to admit that her mother needed emotional support every now and then. She had always thought of her as the rock of the family.

Mona's father, on the other hand, played only a small role in her life. Murida had always emphasized the importance of showing deference for Saleem, which Mona did. But Mona also knew how much her mother suffered from her father's behavior, particularly when he threatened to run away from home or throw himself off the balcony if he didn't get his way. Mona had seen her father placing one leg over the balcony railing, shouting that he wanted to jump to his death.

How frightened she and her siblings had felt! They'd run out and hung on to his other leg, crying for him not to fall, not to die. Years later, Mona realized that he was bluffing; he loved life too much. Yet her mother had always let him win all arguments, so that the family wouldn't be embarrassed. No matter how difficult it made her life, and how much it affected her spirits, Murida always let Saleem get his way.

After sitting a while at the Cedar's restaurant, Murida agreed to go to Mona's house instead of back to her own home. Saleem, they agreed, would come and eat with them in the afternoon. Mona called her father with the plan before driving off with her mother.

Soon, they stepped into Mona's apartment, which was on the fortieth floor of a fashionable Sharjah building. Although Mona had only three children, her apartment was more than double the size of her parents' home in Dubai. They passed through a huge foyer that was furnished like a small living room before they walked into the kitchen, which had enormous windows that looked out onto the tall buildings all around them, as well as a man-made lake with a large fountain.

Mona heated water for instant coffee, and they moved to the casual living room, which also had large windows from which they could see the buildings where Manal and Amal lived on the other side of the lake.

Mona sipped at her Nescafe and set the mug on a coffee table. "Don't you think we should let my sisters know?"

"I told Maha—she's mature and can keep a secret. But the others might not be able to keep it to themselves. And I don't want to deal with their reactions. I have enough to deal with right now. I can barely handle your father."

"Okay"

"Is Mahmoud coming to dinner?"

"I didn't ask him. Would you like me to?"

Murida nodded, and Mona pulled out her phone to call her brother. Murida had to see her son. She needed to show him her love and to make up for not taking his phone call earlier.

Murida had wanted two or three sons, like everyone else, like our sister Muhiba. Who but a good son would support his mother in her old age? Even though her daughters grew into strong women, and always came through for her, Murida never stopped feeling that she'd somehow lost out by having only one son. This made it even more poignant when Mahmoud took Saleem's side over hers.

But even if those slights stung, Murida was always proud of Mahmoud. Although she'd thought that Mahmoud could become a doctor, a career in architecture was great, too. Mahmoud was no less that any of his brothers-in-law, and no one in the extended family could claim superiority over her Mahmoud. *God keep him for me and for his three sons*, Murida frequently thought.

Murida had a soft spot for another boy: her first grandson, Osama. When he was born when she was not yet forty, Murida asked God to protect him at every prayer, just as she had for Mahmoud. Maha was still living in the dorms at al-Ain University when she got married and had Osama, so Murida kept him for a whole year, until Maha finished and took him to two hours away to her apartment in Abu Dhabi. That day was etched in Murida's memory for the rest of her life. She cried like a child as she placed Osama in the car. He cried for her as the car sped away.

Murida was so happy every time Mahmoud's wife delivered a healthy son, and she was glad that her beloved son didn't have any girls. *It's as my mother so often said*, Murida thought: *"A mother's worry about her girls doesn't end until her death."* And Mahmoud's wife was good to him, too. She was intelligent and educated and worked at the best private school in Sharjah.

Murida hadn't known that Mahmoud would become such a strong man, worth two ordinary men. If she'd known, she might have stopped getting pregnant after Mona. Having three children was enough. With Saleem's limited income, they might have lived better. But our mother kept saying, "The next one will be a son, I'm sure," until Murida had five more girls.

How could Mother know? Yes, the neighborhood women had trusted her medical advice. But who could tell if a pregnant woman would have a girl or a boy? Why did Murida listen? Maybe she was counting on God's mercy, or luck, or statistics. She didn't have much in her life, so she thought He would make it up to her by giving her another boy.

Later, Murida decided that God didn't work that way. Our brother Mutasim had four boys—his only girl had died in infancy. And yet he and his wife hadn't suffered so many troubles. Worse, Mutasim's wife could be mean and uncaring towards her children. When Murida had visited her parents in Beirut one summer, she'd seen her sister-in-law's attitude towards her two eldest boys. Mutasim's wife would warm up hotdogs for dinner, give them to the boys, and go back to her bedroom, looking irritated. Hotdogs!

CHAPTER SEVEN

It wasn't long before Mahmoud arrived. He walked straight to his mother and bent down to kiss the back of her hand.

"May God bless you, *habibi*." Murida's voice was thick with emotion. "May He give you a long and happy life"

"How are you, Mother?"

"I'm as good as I can be. Did Mona tell you that it may take five days before we know the results?"

Mahmoud sat down beside his mother. "Yes, but I can talk to Dr. Hasan. You know him—he's the son of the family who lived two houses down from us in the camp."

"Oh, I remember him. Is he already a doctor? The last I saw him, he was a teenager. God bless him for his poor mother and sick father."

"He works in the children's section of the hospital, so he must know someone in x-ray. Should l call him?"

"How well do you know him?"

"Pretty well," Mahmoud said. "He bought an apartment in the last building I designed, and he wanted special touches. I helped him get the materials at a discount."

"Maybe you should call him now?" Mona said.

"I don't have his number, but I can call the building concierge."

Mona nodded.

While his mother and sister sat in the living room, Mahmoud called the concierge and managed to get Dr. Hasan's number. On the phone with the doctor, he explained his mother's condition, asking that Hasan not tell anyone.

Dr. Hasan told Mahmoud that what the technician had said was true. But Dr. Hasan promised that he would talk to them first thing the next morning. He would go in person.

By the time Mahmoud hung up, Murida had understood the gist of the conversation. She smiled. "Thank God. That's better."

Murida's eyes went sparkly, glazed with tears of appreciation for her good luck and the help of her good son. Two days wasn't so bad. She was used to waiting much longer for the results of her annual blood tests. She went every year and got blood work for diabetes, cholesterol, uric acid, and a blood count. She also had an annual urine test to check for infections and albumin. She took good care of her health, even going in for a yearly "female" test, which she hated.

After the rush of emotion, Murida felt tired. She was surprised to be so tired even though she hadn't done any housework. She would soon learn that bad feelings could tire her just as much.

"Mona, can I take a nap in your room?"

"But you haven't eaten. Father will be here any minute now, and then we can eat."

"I don't want to wait."

"Why don't I heat up some chicken and rice, and you take a nap after you eat?"

Murida agreed and, after a small meal, she walked to the master bedroom to pray and rest. Although she loved the large room—which had a huge bed, pictures on the walls, carpet that felt like silk, and a large closet that was big enough for a bedroom—she would come to long for her own small apartment.

That afternoon, Murida slept deeply for the first time since the doctor's visit. She didn't even dream. There was nothing to do any longer but wait.

Mona checked on her mother twice, peering into the master bedroom, and Murida seemed peaceful. *Maybe*, Mona thought, *this is a good sign.*

As the sun was setting, Mona entered the master bedroom and woke her mother. She didn't want to do it, but Mona believed that it wasn't good to sleep through two phases of light: A person could sleep all day, but then they had to wake up before sunset. Mona stood beside her mother's bed for several minutes—it was hard to wake Murida up. She must have been in need of sleep.

When Murida was finally awake, Mona made tea and Murida went back to her chair in the living room. As she sat, she held a pillow clutched to her stomach and chest, looking sad.

Murida's eldest daughter, Maha, lived two hours away from the rest of the family, in Abu Dhabi. On the day of the mammogram, Maha got home from work and immediately called her sister. Maha had known about the lump before everyone else. She'd even known about the retraction of her mother's nipple, but her anxiety had increased after a bad dream the night before the test. She'd dreamt that their mother was flying up to the clouds, smiling, while Maha was calling to her to come back. Maha had woken up frightened, sweaty, her heart racing.

After she heard that the mammogram results would take several days, Maha couldn't eat, or sleep. She was scared. She loved her mother, and she still asked for her mother's advice, just as her mother asked her for advice. Maha wasn't strong like Mona—she admitted that—but it wasn't her fault. She was thin, small, and got sick easily. She hadn't taken good care of her health, just as she hadn't fussed over her appearance. Unlike other girls, she didn't worry endlessly about eyebrows and makeup. She'd mostly cared about being smart at school, and later about being the best Math teacher she could be. She was always at the top of her class and had graduated high school at the very top of the public-school system, sixth in the national exams in the whole country. The Emir himself had handed her a degree, an expensive watch, and a small sum of money. She had framed the picture of the two of them.

Maha had started in engineering, but switched to math at the recommendation of many architects and engineers in the family who thought it would be hard for a mother to be a full-time engineer. While in university, she'd married and had a baby. After graduation, Maha moved away to Abu Dhabi, where her husband worked. There, she found a job in a government school. The pressure was less than at a private school, but the pay was also less.

There, Maha was a popular and well-regarded math teacher, and the parents flocked to her, asking her to tutor their children. But after fifteen years, she wanted to quit. Her job was tiring, and she felt the new generation of kids was nothing like her generation. Most of the children she taught were Emirati, and they were guaranteed a job no matter what sort of education they received. They didn't live like the Arab expatriates, one on top of the other in high buildings. The Emiratis had houses, gardens, and drivers.

But Maha kept working, because her family needed the income. She now had five children to help support through university. She was the only one among her sisters who had worked for this long, but that was her destiny: Her husband was a government accountant with a limited income. Still, he was a very nice man—he was religious in the right way, not like so many who claimed to be religious but whose attitudes and behavior spoke otherwise. She was glad to be married to a kind man like Rafiq.

Maha's married life wasn't completely without troubles: Rafiq had diabetes so severe that it had nearly caused him to go blind. He'd also had several heart attacks that led to heart failure. It frustrated Rafiq that there was so much he couldn't do because of his health. But, unlike Maha's father, Rafiq didn't shout when he got frustrated. Instead, he went to the nearby mosque and prayed.

Maha appreciated her husband's piousness. When she had moved to the UAE as a teenager, she'd been immersed in Islam. Maha absorbed the material deeply, believed it wholeheartedly, and became religious at an early age. She was the first of her sisters to cover her hair, and her three daughters also followed suit, covering their hair when they were still children.

It was deep into the night before Maha fell asleep. Soon after, she woke up to the dawn *adhan* and prayed. After the *shahada*, at the end of prayer, she called on God to protect her mother from all evil, to have the mammogram reveal that Murida didn't have cancer. Maha prayed a few more sets, asking God to forgive her mother of any wrongdoing. She prayed that God would not allow her and her siblings to become orphans; she prayed that He would give her mother patience in dealing with her father; she prayed that He would protect Rafiq from further illness and give each of her children a long, healthy life. After that, Maha went to bed and slept a little. For the moment, the prayer seemed to have cleansed her of bad thoughts.

In the morning, Maha told her husband about her dream. She also told Rafiq that she missed her mother and wanted to visit her in Dubai. Although he was nearly blind, Rafiq could still drive his wife to the taxi station. There, Maha settled into a car for the two-hour trip. She sat on the left side in the back, next to the window. Beside her were two Emirati women who did not speak a word during the entire ride. In the company of strange men, a conservative Emirati woman did not let her voice be heard.

Maha wished she could be at her mother's side immediately. *What a waste of time. Why couldn't Rafiq have a job in Sharjah or Dubai?* Maha had agreed to marry the first man who was presented to her, but she'd hated the idea of going so far away. True, she was still in the same country—her younger sister Hanan had just immigrated all the way to Canada! But the trip from Abu Dhabi was just long enough that she could visit only on special occasions. Her brother and four of her sisters had stayed in Sharjah close to their parents.

Maha would have loved to stay close, but a woman followed her husband to the ends of the earth—at least that's what Maha had heard from older women, including her mother, as well as from certain Muslim scholars. Maha hadn't known that being far from her family would be so difficult. When she'd agreed to marry Rafiq, she'd been young and hadn't really understood the consequences, just as Murida probably hadn't understood the consequences of marrying Saleem.

But, like her mother, Maha grew to accept her destiny. She had complete faith in what God chose for each person. She never felt jealous of her sisters for having more money—from birth, everyone got what was written for him or her. Maha believed in an afterlife where

God would make it up to those who had suffered on earth. She lived with this idea daily, and it eased both her financial struggles and her worries about Rafiq's health. But it didn't seem to relieve her worry about her mother. She couldn't accept the idea of *any* possible reward in heaven that would balance the misery that might be waiting for Murida.

As she rode from Abu Dhabi to Sharjah, Maha thought about her wedding day, which had been full of tears. Maha had cried a flood of them as she'd said good-bye to her parents and each of her siblings. Their Dubai home was small, but she hated leaving its familiar surroundings. Most of all, she'd hated leaving her mother, who loved and respected her so much. They were so close that Murida even allowed herself to complain about Saleem openly and to confide in Maha about private matters.

On the day of her wedding, Maha had thought back on the twenty-one years she'd spent with her family. The first fifteen, they'd been together in the refugee camp in Beirut. The rest they'd spent in their two apartments in Dubai, the first of which had been even more crowded than their home in the camp. And true, the camp house had been crowded, but they'd been so happy! They'd laughed. As long as the children had done well at school, Murida never nagged them. She was never mean like other mothers. Sometimes she would lose her temper after an argument with Saleem, but she never took it out on the kids. Yet Maha couldn't deny that Mother was sometimes mean to Amal.

On her wedding day, Maha had cried more than she'd cried when the whole family had left Lebanon. Back then, she'd still been with her family. But in marrying Rafiq, she was setting out completely on her own. She had to leave Mahmoud, the other "genius" in the family, who also loved math and with whom she'd shared the upstairs room in their refugee-camp home. For the first year after she'd left home, Maha couldn't sleep until she'd called and made sure that Mahmoud was home safely.

Abu Dhabi had always seemed a long way from Dubai. In the coming months of Murida's illness, Maha would feel that the physical distance between Abu Dhabi and Dubai growing ever greater.

It seemed like ages before Maha arrived at the taxi station in Sharjah and called Mona to come pick her up. Mona found Maha standing against a wall, looking out over the street and wearing a black galabiya and black head cover. The sisters exchanged brief greetings and kisses on the cheeks before they got into the car.

"What do you think Mother has?" Maha asked.

Mona wished she knew.

Maha nodded and was silent for a while. "Who knows about this besides you and Mahmoud?"

Mona shook her head. No one knew.

"I'm so scared. I never thought Mother would get cancer."

"Don't say that." Mona turned sharply in her seat. "God willing she won't have it."

"Of course I didn't mean it that way."

Mona was silent for a moment. As she stopped at a busy intersection, she asked her sister "So did you tell Rafiq?"

"No. I said I had a bad dream about Mother, and that's why I needed to see her. Which is true—the dream, I mean."

"I had to tell Khaled. He just wouldn't believe that there was nothing wrong with me, I've been so worried. But he won't tell anyone, I know."

"I don't know how I'm going to feel when I see Mother," Maha said. "I don't know if I can keep from crying."

"You shouldn't cry."

Maha nodded, although she could already feel that she wouldn't be as strong as her younger sister. She just couldn't.

The drive to the family home didn't take long.

This was Murida and Saleem's second apartment in Dubai, on the second floor of a squat, two-story building. They'd moved to the new apartment in November 1978, a year after they'd arrived in the Emirates. It was in this apartment that they raised their seven children. The building was ugly in comparison to the other tall, ornate buildings in Sharjah and Dubai. But it was solid, identical to all the others in the large public-housing complex.

As in the other buildings all around, the ground level was two feet above street level. But most of these buildings lacked proper stairs. Instead, each had a single, large cinderblock step so that residents and visitors could clamber up to the building's entrance.

When I'd visited my sister there in 1982, in order to shake off the ugly events of that summer when the Israeli military invaded Lebanon and expelled the PLO, it had been hard to get up into the entryway with my crutch. Still, once I was inside, the whole family had been full of joy, dancing, and singing. I'd slept on a mattress in the living room, but I didn't mind. Although the family home was small, it was full of Murida's warmth.

When Mona and Maha arrived, Murida opened the door with a smile on her face, but all three of them could tell it was a fake smile. Yes, her lips were stretched, but her eyes couldn't lie. *Why is she bothering to fake a smile?* Maha asked herself. *We're not strangers.* But that's how her mother was—she didn't want to overburden her daughters. She knew they were upset and confused, just like her. She exchanged kisses with both of them, and all three went into the living room.

Murida sat down. "How did you explain it to Rafiq, about wanting to come on such short notice?"

Maha told her mother not to worry. She just wanted to know how she was doing.

"I don't feel bad. The only thing is that the night sweats have come back. You remember how I told you that, for about six months now, I feel warm at night and wake up soaking in sweat?"

"I thought the doctor said there was nothing wrong with you", Maha said.

"Yes, I went to the doctor three months ago, and she said there was nothing wrong, that my temperature was only thirty-eight degrees. But last night, I felt it again."

"Once we know the result of the mammogram, we'll ask Dr. Sandhir about the sweating." Mona looked towards her sister and their eyes met. Each read the other's mind: Why hadn't this earlier doctor detected the lump? Maybe she hadn't examined Murida's breasts.

After a short pause, Maha looked into her mother's face. "How has Father been so far?"

"Okay so far. I doubt he thinks about it very much."

"Well, maybe that's for the best."

Murida nodded and asked Mona if she wanted to make tea or coffee, but neither Maha nor Mona felt like a hot drink.

After a short period of silence, Maha spoke. "Can I do my prayer in your room? It's getting a little late for the noon prayer."

"Of course, God bless you and reward you for all your prayers." Murida turned her gaze to Mona. "Don't you want to pray, too?"

"I will after Maha."

Maha got up and looked at her mother briefly before she went to her parents' bedroom, where she stretched out her mother's prayer rug. Murida had bought it from Mecca during her *hajj*. It had the picture of the Ka'aba, which Murida had so admired. She'd loved it so much that she hadn't wanted to share it, and Saleem agreed to keep the old rug.

As Maha stood at the edge of the small rug, and before she'd said a single word, she felt herself being taken back through the years, through all the times her mother's feet had been placed on this soft surface, five times a day. The new feeling was powerful, but Maha couldn't grasp it right away. She felt both scared and privileged to be in her mother's place, praying to their creator. And it wasn't just those two feelings: There was so much more in her heart that she couldn't identify. Silently, she groped toward understanding. She'd never felt this closeness to her mother, as if one of them could not exist without the other. Why now?

Even though Maha's mind wasn't clear, she went on to pray. She hated that she wasn't in complete harmony with her Creator during this prayer. She usually surrendered herself completely—that was how the scholars said prayer should be. But she forgave herself, knowing that today was not a usual day. She believed that God would forgive her, too.

Once she was finished praying, Maha forced herself to stay kneeling, as if to experience her surrender to God a little longer. When Maha finally finished her prayer, she went back and sat beside her mother on the two-seat sofa. The room was silent, as Maha didn't know what to say. Maha wondered how, after forty-four years of being so close, there could be a barrier now? It must be fear, Maha thought. Maha's inner life was so connected with her mother's that she never thought of herself without her mother.

CHAPTER EIGHT

Finally, it was Saturday morning. On Friday night, Murida had asked Mahmoud to call her the *second* he heard from Dr. Hasan. He'd said that he would, but in truth he planned to rush out and pick up Mona if he heard bad news. The two of them would go to their parents' home together and tell their mother. They both agreed that they shouldn't share bad news on the phone.

At ten in the morning, Murida's doorbell rang. When she opened the door and saw Mona and Mahmoud standing in the hallway, she felt suddenly light-headed and unsteady. *It must be bad news. They would've called if it was good news.*

Murida cleared her throat. "Why didn't you call?"

"We wanted to come anyway," Mona said. She and Mahmoud walked into the apartment and closed the door behind them.

Murida looked at them, expectantly.

"Dr. Hasan called me about an hour ago." Mahmoud said. "He said he looked at the test with the specialist, and they saw a lump. But it isn't clear what type of lump it is."

"Don't lie to me. Tell me the truth."

"I swear that's all," Mahmoud said. "Dr. Hasan said you need a biopsy."

Mahmoud was already lying to his mother. Dr. Hasan said the radiologist was almost certain it was cancer. But almost cancer wasn't the same as cancer, Mahmoud thought, so he felt he was only partly lying.

"Okay." Murida turned to her daughter. "Mona, get me an appointment at the Iranian hospital. It's less expensive."

"It's not about the money," Mahmoud said.

"They say that it's a good hospital. Besides, it's close."

Mona stepped away to make her calls. She got an appointment for the following day. Somehow, the surgeon who did breast biopsies had an opening at eight in the morning.

The biopsy was a big event in Murida's life, as she'd never before needed surgery. The only previous medical trauma had been her single miscarriage. Since her birth in Palestine, Murida had been healthy and strong. As a five-year-old girl, she'd even walked some of the way out of Palestine when, in October 1948, her family had fled air bombardment of their town. Although the townspeople had stayed throughout the weeks of ground fighting, they had no weapons against the airplanes. Once in Beirut, Murida had never tired of doing the housework for her mother. When Muhiba was pregnant, Murida even carried water to Muhiba's home. She'd delivered her seven children with no adverse physical effects.

Unlike our mother, Murida was not a hypochondriac, and unlike our older sister Muhiba, she didn't have psychosomatic symptoms. Murida was careful with her health and took good care of her body. If Murida had a complaint, everyone knew there had to be a good reason. In the previous ten years her hearing had suffered, and she'd gone to many specialists, all of whom confirmed there was no treatment. Her difficulty hearing made Murida feel ashamed, especially when Muhiba had stung her once by asking "Are you deaf?" at a large family gathering. Murida had felt the sting twice over: once for being addressed so sharply, and again because it came from her sister, who had never seemed to accept her as an equal.

The surgeon who did the biopsy the next morning was a middle-aged Iranian man.

He had white hair and a thin white beard, and Murida found him very kind and respectful. He even spoke good Arabic. *He must be a Muslim*, my sister thought. After he explained the procedure, a nurse took Murida to another wing of the hospital. Mona and Mahmoud were worried for their mother. Before this, they'd never had to think about her health.

But Mona and Mahmoud didn't have to wait for long—the procedure went by in a flash. One short hour after Murida was wheeled away, she was wheeled back to the waiting area by another nurse. She'd wanted to walk back, but the nurse had insisted that these were hospital rules.

Murida hated to be seen in a wheelchair. After all, she wasn't a cripple. Whenever she'd seen me at the airport being pushed in a wheelchair, she'd always felt sorry for me, and when a neighbor once referred to me as "your brother, the cripple," Murida got very upset. As soon as she was in the waiting room, Murida got out of the wheelchair, and she and her children went home.

Mona and Mahmoud had been told to expect results in about a week. Murida told her children that she didn't have any pain, and she didn't remember the procedure, either. No, she felt no pain at all—which, as she thought about it, seemed strange.

Murida hadn't always felt unlucky. When Mahmoud was born, just two years after Murida got married, she'd felt fortunate. She had her first son after only one girl. Our mother, by contrast, had suffered through four girls before delivering a boy, and Muhiba had birthed two girls before Khaled was born. Murida must be lucky! If she had three more pregnancies, she thought, one or two might be boys.

At twenty, Murida felt blessed at last, after so many difficulties in her life. Yes, her son Mahmoud was brownish like her, which was a mark against him in 1960s Beirut, especially since her nephew Khaled was as blonde as some Western movie stars. But Mahmoud was handsome, and so intelligent and eager to learn. He always crowded his sister Maha while she did home-work, wanting to know what she was learning. Murida was so worried about Mahmoud getting an illness or into an accident. He was her prize—or he would be, she thought, until the second boy arrived to share his glory.

Mahmoud called the hospital on the fifth day and ev-ery day after. Early on, he learned to ask for the pathol-ogy department, but he still got nowhere. Every time, a different person answered the phone and, every time, the person who answered seemed equally baffled. Mahmoud never got a clear answer about his mother's results or when to expect them.

Diya Mutasim M.D.

On the seventh day, Mahmoud went in person. He was shocked to learn that they had no sample from his mother. After all, the Iranian Hospital was supposed to be highly regarded. But as he made his way past the waiting room to the offices and labs, Mahmoud saw chaos and mess. The staff was giggling, speaking in Persian, and appeared to be moving around aimlessly. As Mahmoud walked around looking for his mother's results, he felt increasingly angry and helpless. He lost his temper, began shouting at the assistants, and demanded to see the director. A young woman in a full headscarf came over, but she was of no use. She had no record of receiving a specimen from a Murida Mutasim.

Mahmoud was furious. *Seven days wasted*, he thought. *Who was responsible?* Was it the doctor who did the biopsy, the nurse who was supposed to make sure the specimen got to the right place, or the lab that should've received the specimen and performed the test? What would he tell his mother? Mahmoud could not leave the hospital like this. As long as he was in the hospital, he had a chance for a miracle. Once he left, he had to admit that hope was completely gone. Eventually, he gave up and left the hospital, angry and despondent, wishing he wasn't Palestinian, wasn't a person with no nationality and no rights, with no institution he could call on for help.

Mahmoud had never felt this helpless before. He couldn't think of any way to break the news to his mother. He called Dr. Hasan, who told him that Murida should have the whole lump removed, preferably at a private hospital.

With this advice, Mahmoud felt a little better. It was a good idea—he'd tell his mother that the sample was too small to interpret accurately. It would be another partial lie, but Murida would believe it. After all, she'd commented after the biopsy that she'd been shocked at how tiny the wound was.

As Mahmoud expected, Murida was disappointed and hurt when she heard that the sample was too small. But, more than that, she was angry. She wished she could shout and empty her heart of all the frustration that had built up over the past few weeks. But she couldn't. Women didn't do that; they kept their feelings to themselves. Men had the privilege of raising their voices. Murida wished, on that morning, that she'd been born a man. She had the strength and determination that were supposed to be the providence of men. She could've gone to college and gotten a degree like any man, like her brothers. Or she could've run a small company, like her father.

Fortunately, with the help of the kind Dr. Hasan, Murida got an appointment two days later with a good surgeon. Finally, Murida thought, they were moving forward toward a resolution.

Throughout her life, Murida had rarely asked for help. She knew it was possible that her brothers would help her financially if she needed it. But she would never ask us.

Our father hadn't waited to be asked. When he'd wanted to, he'd stepped in and lent Murida a hand. He loved his second-oldest daughter, and he always told her how proud he was of the strength she'd shown in dealing with life's difficulties. He'd been proud of her ever since she was their uncomplaining child-house-keeper. As she grew up, our father had been proud of how she'd handled her relationship with Saleem.

Murida knew that our father resented our mother for acting weak and sickly. He liked strong, determined people. There was no other way for Palestinian refugees, he always said, adding: When you don't have a country, you lose all dignity, and you can count only on your own two hands and your money to help you survive.

Our father, who had been a farmer in Palestine, worked hard: first as a stone mason, and later as a contractor, building a business from nothing. It was true that most of his money had gone to the education of his sons and creating a new building far from the camp. But he'd also made money for Murida and Muhiba by investing their savings in shares of an apartment in his building. He'd sold their shares and doubled their money after only a few months.

Murida loved our mother, but she resembled our father. She loved Father's smile—it was rare, but that made it all the more special. She even looked more like Father. They both had thick lips, which was an undesirable trait at the time, and dark brown eyes. But Murida didn't get our father's straight hair. Instead, she had curly hair like our mother, another undesirable trait for Arab girls in those years.

Yet, as much as she loved him, Murida didn't want to meet Father yet. She wanted to live a little longer. Then, at the right time, she would be happy to see him, surely in heaven.

CHAPTER NINE

The second time, the surgeon was a Lebanese man who spoke with Murida for few minutes before they wheeled her to the operating room. He was charming and kept saying "everything will be okay." Murida felt reassured that he *must* be better than the Iranian doctor. The last thing she remembered was counting numbers. When Murida woke after surgery to the sounds of several people talking at the same time, she felt a little nauseous. Her mouth was dry, and her mind foggy. This state of mind felt like an improvement. Although she couldn't think straight, she also couldn't be tense, sad, or worried.

As soon as Murida regained her mental strength, she looked at the left side of her chest and noticed a large dressing. This time, there was sharp pain. *The surgeon must have removed the whole thing,* Murida thought with relief. *I am free of the lump. Maybe this really is the end.*

Could it be this easy? Murida stared at the dressing and wondered. *Maybe I'll have kafta or shawarma tonight. I can ask Mahmoud to bring it. They say that hospital food is tasteless, and I haven't enjoyed food for more than two weeks.* The nurse came over to the bed and asked if Murida needed anything. Just water, Murida said.

The nurse brought her ice water, but Murida wanted her drink at room temperature. She told the nurse that ice water would give her a sore throat. Murida didn't know yet, but her relationship to food and drink would change dramatically in the coming months.

Before this, Murida had loved food. She was five when our family arrived in Beirut. In the first years, before our family moved to the camp, ten people were crowded into one apartment. Along with our own immediate family, there was an uncle, two aunts and our grandparents, all on Father's side. Food must've been scarce, and she was a child competing with adults. Two years later, after they'd moved to the camp, Murida acquired a liking for food of all kinds, including the dishes that she helped her mother make. When Murida moved out after her wedding, she would cook nearly every day for the rest of her life.

Murida couldn't afford meat or chicken regularly, especially once she had nine mouths to feed. But her children never complained.

Back in the waiting area, a nurse informed Saleem, Mahmoud, and Mona that Murida was recovering well, and they could see her as soon as she was transferred to a regular room. They all thanked the nurse effusively, as if she'd had something to do with Murida's well-being. This was tradition. It was not so with the bearer of bad news, who might even deserve to be punished.

Saleem sniffed. "I told you she'd be fine. *Allah kbeer*, God is great."

Mahmoud and Mona didn't feel like talking. They just wanted to see their mother.

Finally, they were shown to Room 222, where Murida occupied the first of two beds. She was propped up and looked serene. *It must be the anesthesia*, Mona thought. For two weeks, Murida had not looked this relaxed.

As Murida drifted in and out of her sleepy state, Mona noticed that, in the second bed, there was an older woman who didn't appear at all ill. Mona smiled widely every time her eyes met those of the older woman. She soon learned that the older woman was recovering from gallbladder surgery. She was a kind-spirited

Emirati, and she told Mona about how she'd grown up in the desert before all the buildings had gone up, before the wealth of her country had become known across the globe, and before they filled the skyline with tall buildings as if they wanted to reach God.

She was happier back then, living in the desert with camels and goats. Life was simpler, the woman said, and people didn't get sick as much. Food was healthier, not like the present, when children preferred to eat greasy, so-called "fast food."

"These things are against our traditions and against the Prophet's teachings," the woman told Mona. "The West is exporting bad food, just as they exported bad music, bad clothing, and bad ideas. It's all about money for the Emir, but money never bought happiness. That comes with faith, good deeds, and good intentions."

Mona nodded in agreement the whole time.

"On the contrary," the woman added. "Money brings many ills."

"Where are your children?" Mona asked.

"I have only one child. My husband died very young, but I was fortunate to have a son. He was only two when his father was found dead—no one knew how my husband died. But when they brought him home to me, he had a smile on his face. I wondered: How could someone die while smiling?"

"He must have smiled at meeting his Creator," Mona said.

"He was such a good man. Our fathers were brothers, and I was promised to him the moment I was born."

"Let me be your daughter. What can I get you?"

"Nothing," the woman said. "God give you strength for your mother's sake. If I had a daughter, I would like her to be like you, so kind and religious, and pretty."

As Mona and the woman talked, Murida moved in and out of a sleepy, peaceful state. When they left the hospital, Mona and Mahmoud hoped that their mother would be back to her old self soon. They missed old Murida.

Saleem also wanted Murida to be her old self. He wanted the present to end and the recent past to return—he didn't care how. It was *hard* to act kindly all the time, and he'd held back his temper for several weeks now. What would happen if he couldn't get angry for a very long time? It would likely affect his health, Saleem thought. Internal anger had to "come out," or else it could hurt a man's health. It could show up as heart trouble. But he couldn't yell at Murida now—she might have cancer. His children, especially Mahmoud, would shun him. So Saleem prayed that his wife would get well soon.

For the first time, Saleem admitted to himself that Murida had been his support for all these years. He couldn't imagine himself in a world where she didn't exist. She tolerated his temper, so—he thought—she must love him. Did he love her? He had no idea, and he didn't know where to begin with these sorts of questions. He'd never desired another woman, and he knew that she was always there for him—that she *should* be always there for him.

It was a while before Murida felt fully awake. When she did, she wanted to know how the procedure had gone. "Did they say when we'll know the results?"

Mahmoud stepped forward toward his mother. "Dr. Hasan said it takes at least three work days. He'll look into it for us and let me know."

"Please thank him for all his help."

Mahmoud agreed, and offered to get his mother some food from a restaurant.

"No, the nurse said I can eat only soft food tonight. It's late now, so why don't you all go home?" Murida paused. "Where is your father?"

"He's socializing with the Filipino nurses," Mona said. "I saw him at the nurses' station, offering them candy."

"Mahmoud, can you take him to sleep at your house tonight?"

Mahmoud nodded, and Mona walked up to the other side of her mother's bed. "Can we tell my sisters? If they found out on their own that you were at the hospital, they'd be so disappointed and scared."

"Okay. But tell them it was for a biopsy, not a lumpectomy. And don't let any of them visit tonight. Not yet."

Murida's husband and two children left, each with their own thoughts, hopes, and burdens. On the way back, Saleem asked what was for dinner. Mahmoud told him there was stuffed cabbage, and Saleem asked if they could pick up shawarma sandwiches or roast chicken instead.

Before getting the food, Mahmoud dropped Mona off at her house—she wanted to be back with her children. She needed to spend time with Tala, her fourteen-year-old daughter and close friend. Tala had been tense lately, and Mona imagined it was in response to her own changing moods. After all, Tala knew her mother too well to miss reading her emotions.

Tala had always been special in her grandmother Murida's eyes. *Teyta* had always called Tala the pretty one. She'd remarked on Tala's thick dark hair, black eyes with snow-white sclera, long eyelashes, and small lips—all traditional hallmarks of Palestinian beauty.

Indeed, Murida had special affection for Tala, who was socially confident from a young age and kind and caring well beyond her years. Tala was highly perceptive of people's feelings, even those of adults, and she gave affection as much as she received it. Murida thought her granddaughter was unusual for a girl of her generation.

Tala, for her part, thought her grandmother—her *teyta*—was an angel. Tala knew from her mother's stories that Murida had gone through a lot. As for the relationship between her grandparents, no one had to tell Tala how difficult her grandfather could be. She'd witnessed it many times. Tala resented that her society permitted such behavior—men weren't better than women, after all. They complemented one another. Each needed the other to carry out God's plan for humanity on this earth.

Tala wasn't prepared for her grandmother's illness, but she would do her best to show her grandmother that she was loved.

Tala would soon be brought in to help. After the lumpectomy, Mona couldn't keep her worries from her daughter any longer. She needed Tala by her side. Unlike her brothers, Tala didn't need any prompting to study—she was independent and proud. She would become important one day, Mona thought. She could be a doctor, or an engineer like her father and uncle Mahmoud.

Around four o'clock, Mona got home, set down her bag, and pulled off her shoes. Then she went immediately to find her daughter. "How are you, *habibti* Tala?"

"Good. I just got here, maybe fifteen minutes ago."

"Can we go to the kitchen table? I want to make a Nescafe."

Tala knew that her mother had something to tell her. It was obvious from her mother's eyes and from the tone of her voice. She followed her mother slowly into the kitchen, where Mona heated water and got down a mug. After a minute, she sat down at the table, and Tala sat at the edge of a chair.

"Your grandmother is at the hosp—"

Before Mona could finish the sentence, Tala gave an explosive cry.

"I knew something was wrong. I thought it was you. What's wrong with Teyta?"

"We don't know yet. She had a small lump removed from her breast this morning."

Tala was breathing heavily and put her hands to her mouth. "So it could be bad. Oh my God not Teyta, no" She brought a hand sharply down against the table. "Where is she now?"

"At the Ajman hospital, but just for tonight. We'll take her home tomorrow."

"I want to be with her. I can miss school tomorrow."

"You don't have to, *habibti*."

"Yes, I have to. Tomorrow is a light day and I can manage. I have to be with Teyta."

Tala knew that she would have to appear strong in front of Murida. She had to act as a source of support and not a burden—it was her turn to pay Teyta back for all she'd done: sewing Tala beautiful dresses like those in European magazines, caring for Tala when she was sick with the flu, and so much more. What's more, Tala had to honor the privilege of being the only granddaughter who knew about the surgery.

Tala thought about how she would spoil her grandmother. She would be her nurse, and she would be proud to change her dressing. As soon as Teyta was here, Tala would sit by her and wrap her arms around her neck. Tala loved her grandmother's smell, of food and peace, and Teyta had loved it when Tala had wrapped her arms around her, as if she were still a small child.

But Tala was afraid, too. She'd never been to a hospital before. She wasn't sure how she would feel around so much illness and death. Could she hold in her feelings when her eyes meet her grandmother's? She knew she had to. She would do her best.

CHAPTER TEN

The next morning, Tala and her mother drove to the hospital to pick up Murida. Seeing her grandmother at the hospital was much harder than Tala had expected, especially as the nurse insisted on wheeling Murida out to Mona's car. Murida objected, but again, this was hospital policy. Tala hated seeing her grandmother in a wheelchair just as much as Murida hated being in one. Tala knew how proud Teyta was, and she understood why Teyta was looking down into her lap, hiding her face so that her gaze didn't meet her daughter's or granddaughter's.

Once Murida was safely in the back seat of the car, Tala asked if she could ride in the back seat alongside her. Murida nodded, granting her granddaughter's wish without question. Murida had said so many *nos* to her own children that she couldn't refuse any of her grandchildren's wishes. Besides, she loved to be near Tala. She wished she'd treated her own children as kindly as she now did her grandchildren—but those were difficult times, so she forgave herself.

"*Keefik,* Teyta?"

"Fine, my dear," Murida answered. "You should not have skipped school."

"It was a short day today, and no tests."

The ride back to Mona's apartment was easy—by eleven o'clock, morning traffic had long since ended. All of them were thinking about *cancer.* Until a few weeks before, Murida had always seen cancer as something that affected other people. She'd never thought that it could touch her. They said cancer ran in certain families, and her family didn't have it. Waleed's cancer, in Murida's mind, was an aberration. Who got colon cancer at nineteen?

Murida worried about high blood pressure, yes. She worried about diabetes and kidney diseases, and she checked herself for these every year. She spent her own money to get tested, and she never regretted it. But she'd never thought of checking for cancer. None of her sisters had.

No one had ever told her to get tested—none of her doctors, and not me, even though I knew how careful she was with her health. I knew how she'd lost more than thirty pounds when she learned that being overweight could increase the chance of diabetes and high blood pressure. I knew that she never cooked with fat, but instead with oil, and how she never ate fried food. I even knew that she watched all the health and nutritional advice given on Emirati TV, and followed it avidly. But they had never mentioned breast cancer.

Once they arrived, getting into Mona's building was easy. Unlike her parents' home, Mona's ground floor was only a single, easy step above the street. The small lobby was bright and clean, as were the elevators. The doorman even stood up when they entered.

Once they got inside, Murida drank a little water from the kitchen tap and went to lie down. Tala walked with her and sat at the edge of the bed. She had to do her best to take her grandmother's mind off her illness, and, since she didn't know what to say, she just smiled. She wished Teyta would ask her to do something: brush her hair, make her tea, or go down to get her candy. Teyta loved big, thick chocolate bars. But even though it was only noon, all Teyta wanted was to sleep. The night before, she'd woken up often. The nurses must have checked on her every hour or two.

While Murida slept, Tala went out. Meanwhile, Mona called Maha. "We need to tell our sisters about Mother's condition."

"Do you think Amal can keep a secret?" Maha asked. "You know how she is—impulsive."

"We can't tell some and not all."

"True. Maybe she'll surprise us and keep the secret."

The sisters divided the phone calls, and afterwards they felt relieved of the burden of secrecy and guilt, at least for the moment.

Amal was born in 1970, nine years after Murida married Saleem. She was the fourth daughter, and the first to look and act like her father. She was darker-skinned than some of her other sisters, which was considered "unlucky," and had big dark eyes and a wide forehead. Like her father, she spoke loudly, as if with an effort to ensure she was heard, even if no one else was talking. And like Saleem, she didn't seem to know when to stop talking.

Before Amal was born, Murida had believed our mother's prediction that this fifth child would be a boy. Mother claimed she could tell baby's sex from the shape of the woman's abdomen. Although she had been wrong before, Murida also thought it *must* be time for a boy after three girls. After all, God was fair, or that's what she'd learnt about the God of Muslims. So she was shocked when the midwife uttered the gender of the baby: a girl. Now, Murida had five children under eight to feed, bathe, and watch over. And four of them were girls.

As Amal grew up, she continued to have some of her father's traits. She wasn't as good in school as Mona and Maha, except in math, which was the easiest subject for all Murida's children. Murida found herself yelling at Amal more easily than at her other children. She reprimanded herself every time she did, as it wasn't Amal's fault that she was different.

Murida had doubted the day would ever come, but one afternoon a couple visited Murida and asked for Amal's hand. So Amal got married to a jovial, short young man, a civil engineer, a graduate of the esteemed AUB. His family was also from the village of Tarshiha, in Palestine, and they had lived in the same refugee camp where Murida and Saleem had made their first home. The groom's mother knew our mother Fawziyya well, and felt Murida must be an equally good mother, raising excellent daughters.

Murida was delighted. After the two were married, the young man had one business success after another. Fahmi was smart, affable, and rapidly getting rich. He loved Amal, too. The two seemed like a match made in heaven. He never yelled at Amal, but instead supported her in starting her own small business. He was as generous of spirit as he was generous with money. They had three boys and a girl, and all were bright and did well in school. Despite the times her mother had yelled at her, Amal treated her mother with extra love and respect. Like her husband, it seemed she couldn't hold a grudge.

By the time Murida woke up at five and asked for tea, all her daughters knew what was happening. Tala made the tea and carried it in a mug on a plate along with cookies that she'd bought while her grandmother slept.

Murida rearranged herself in bed and took hold of the mug. "God bless you, *habibti*."

Once Murida was fully awake, Mona told her mother that all her daughters would be coming soon. Murida was relieved to know that all her children had been told about the procedure and, after her short nap, she didn't mind seeing them. She hadn't thought much about them lately, and now she felt guilty and missed them. Before this, her children had never left her mind for more than a few fleeting hours.

Amal, Manal, and Ghina all arrived within few minutes of each other. Amal and Manal were accompanied by their husbands, but Ghina was alone: Her husband worked two hours away and came home only on weekends.

So they told their husbands after all, Murida thought. *That's fine. They're all good men.*

The girls kissed their mother on the cheeks, more times than they usually would at a casual visit. It was their way of expressing extra love for their mother. The men greeted her with warm words.

As everyone moved into the living room, Murida was suddenly aware of the bliss of having all these visitors around. Yes, she was a private person, but all the people in this room cared for her. Murida let herself receive their kindnesses without feeling self-pity. Before this, my strong sister had never admitted that she needed the affection of others. But now she found herself not only accepting the affection, but finding pleasure in it. She was, after all, human.

In order to take her mind off disease, Murida's daughters and sons-in-law talked about the day's news: how cautious they were in investing in the Dubai stock market; how stocks and apartments were overvalued; how expensive things had become. Later, they turned on the TV, and Mona made coffee and tea.

The surgeon had told Mahmoud that he'd removed the whole mass plus two centimeters all around it. So, they reasoned, even if it were cancer, it should be over with: cleared, maybe even cured. That wasn't enough to reassure Murida. She didn't want to have cancer, *period*. She could give up her whole breast if the diagnosis would be "not cancer." She would take any chronic disease as long as it wasn't cancer. Even if her cancer was curable, she just didn't want to be a "cancer victim." Her children, on the other hand, were relieved to think that, if it were cancer, it had been totally removed.

Murida had never liked the idea of being a "victim." She was just five when the status was foist on her the first time, when our family fled Palestine. My parents and three oldest sisters headed first to Aleppo, in northern Syria, on a freight train that also carried sheep. The winter was so harsh that they soon moved on to Lebanon, leaving behind an aunt and a half-uncle who would settle in Aleppo. One uncle married and stayed in Damascus. Another uncle ended up in Amman, Jordan. When not on the train, Murida took turns walking and being carried by our father. Our younger sister Inaam was carried by Mother.

Murida was barely noticed in the crowded Beirut apartment where they lived for two years before the money nearly ran out. After moving to the camp, Murida worked day and night in the house without being patted on the back by her parents. Still, Murida would never have wanted to see herself as a victim.

We—Murida's brothers and sisters—didn't show her much love, either. When my oldest brother Mutasim would hit her, she'd be told to not react. He'd done the same with Muhiba and Inaam, and all were expected not to respond. Mutasim was an active boy, they were told. His sisters in particular were supposed to care for him. Muhiba would occasionally complain, but Murida never did.

Muhiba, the eldest, had always acted with more confidence than Murida. She acted as if she was too good for such a poor, hardscrabble life, as if she was better than her two sisters. Murida was happy when Muhiba left after she married at seventeen, even though it meant Murida had to take on even more work.

CHAPTER ELEVEN

It took nine days before they knew the results of the pathology examination.

In the meantime, Murida's children went back to their recently modified lives and tried to avoid thinking about "the disease." Anyway, the surgeon had said he took it all out. As for my sister, she slowly eased back into a new routine at her daughter Mona's house. Saleem, on the other hand, became agitated at being away from his apartment. Four days of recovery at Mona's house were more than enough, he insisted. He missed his home and the Dubai friends.

On the fifth day after the surgery, Saleem was in Mona's kitchen, watching her heat water for instant coffee, when he gave vent to his thoughts. "Your mother and I should go back home today."

"Why don't you go back and sleep at home if you want?" Mona asked with a look of surprise. "Then you can come and eat with us whenever you like."

"It's not about food," Saleem said. "Is that all you think I care about?"

"No, but Mother is better off here. You know that if she goes home she'll start cleaning and cooking again, and then maybe she won't heal as well. What do you want to do at home?"

"It's my home. And hers, too."

"I know. But you're almost never there except to eat and sleep. If you like, you can take a taxi and go see your friends there. Or Amal's driver can take you." Amal and her husband had an Indian driver.

Saleem looked surprised at being challenged, then disgusted. He was not used to this sort of talk from his daughters, but Mona went on. What she cared about in that moment was her mother's wellbeing.

"You spend your days walking around and visiting with your friends. We're happy that you have so many friends. But Mother has only us, her children"

"What do you mean 'only you'? What about me?"

"Of course you, too. So, if you wish, you can sleep at home and eat here or at Mahmoud's. Or you can get carry-out. Why do you need Mother to go with you?"

"She's my wife, and I'm her husband."

Mona turned away from her father. "Let me call Mahmoud. Maybe he can talk with you—I just don't understand you."

"Don't bother Mahmoud. He's working."

"But he wouldn't agree with you. He cares about Mother's health."

"Are you saying I don't?" Saleem shouted. "I love her."

"Okay then," Mona said. "Do what you wish and let her recover here."

"None of you cares about me." Saleem turned and stormed out, slamming the front door.

Mona was so mad that she wanted to shout at her father. But she knew she'd regret it—he'd go tell the whole world that his own daughter had yelled at him. Plus, Murida wouldn't accept the idea of her children yelling at Saleem. In the coming months, Saleem would want more and more to go back to his "normal" life.

My sister had always worked hard to keep things normal in the house, and to make sure the kids acted respectfully toward their father. It wasn't always easy, particularly when Saleem frightened them with threats that he would kill himself. Murida knew he could never do it. He loved life far too much.

When the family had arrived in Dubai, they'd had to live for the first year in a tiny efficiency in a distant neighborhood full of poor Indian migrant laborers, with many men to a room. After a while, they'd moved to a two-bedroom apartment, where there was one bedroom for Saleem, Murida, and baby Ghina, and another for the five other girls. Mahmoud had to sleep out in the living room, on a mattress that was kept against a wall in the bedroom during the day.

They could've had a pleasant life in that apartment. But in all their years of marriage, Saleem had never let Murida win an argument, even though everyone knew she was the smarter of the two. Still, she never complained, at least not while the children were in the house. She kept all the pain and anger bundled up inside her heart, and sometimes she wondered if that might not be a cause of her occasional bouts with anxiety and sadness.

Still, she never let herself grow very angry with Saleem. She just thought: That's how he is. And she couldn't leave, because where would she go? And what would happen to the girls? Throughout her life, Murida kept one priority before all others: the happy futures of her children.

A week after the procedure, Murida did as Saleem wanted. She went back home. Yet now she didn't stay all day in the apartment: She visited Amal on the first day, Ghina on the second, and Manal on the third. She spent most of the days with her daughters.

While Murida was at Manal's, Mona found herself shopping close to Mahmoud's. She saw her brother's car outside, so she stopped in at his apartment. It was mid-afternoon, during the long break that was customary in the hot Gulf countries. She asked if Mahmoud had heard from the surgeon. He hadn't, so he went into his bedroom and called the surgeon's office, just as he'd done each of the past four days. Apparently, the surgeon had just received the report. When Mahmoud returned from the bedroom, he looked pale, as if he'd grown suddenly ill. Mona didn't need to ask—she could guess what the doctor had said.

Mona stood up and shuddered. "How will we tell her?"

"I don't know. I don't think I can look into her face and tell her. She's started acting almost normal these last few days. I can't give her the news now. I'll have a nervous breakdown looking into her eyes."

Although everyone, including Murida, suspected that this was a case of breast cancer, it was still hard to face the truth. To break the news to their mother would be one of the hardest things they had to do. Mona sat back down on the couch to think. "What if we asked Uncle Diya to tell her? He's a doctor, so he can do it the right way."

"That's a good idea. It's early in the States now. I hope I can get ahold of him and ask him to call Mother."

Mahmoud paced around the room as he called. First, he called my wife at home, and she gave him my office number. At the time, I was in my office at the University of Cincinnati, where I was chair of the dermatology department. When Mahmoud called, I was meeting with my business administrator, but I quickly asked to be alone. My nephew called only when he had serious news. The last time had been two years earlier, when his father-in-law was dying of a heart attack.

I asked my nephew why they hadn't told me about the lump earlier.

"You know how private she is," Mahmoud said. "She didn't want to tell anyone before she knew the results."

I listened to Mahmoud's news and agreed that I could be the one to tell Murida. "How long should I wait before calling at Manal's?"

"Just give us thirty minutes."

A world away from me, Mona tapped her brother's arm and shook her head. "We have to tell our sisters first, so that they're all there. Have him call in an hour."

I'm ten years younger than Murida, which means I was eight when she married Saleem. Even though I was old enough, I don't have any memories of Murida while she still lived at home. Murida did much of the housework, but mostly it was Mother who cared for me, ever since I contracted polio as a toddler. Playing with me was Inaam's job, as she was only five years older.

But I have many memories of visiting Murida soon after I went to university. In good weather, I would climb to the second floor, where she and Saleem had an open space for eating or gathering in hot weather. I would lean on the edge of the steps, where Murida had planted flowers and herbs to bring a little color and sweetness into the ugly camp environment. I often shared a meal with my nieces and nephew in the open space upstairs. I wasn't like their other uncle Mutasim. Instead, I acted silly and made the children laugh. But, like Mutasim, I often told Murida how amazingly smart Mahmoud and Maha were. Knowledge came to them intuitively.

When Murida left Beirut in November 1977, I was almost twenty-five and soon to be a doctor and I surprised the whole family with my emotional good-bye, sobbing and hugging Murida and refusing to let her go. I had just started to know her and love her—I didn't want to let her go so quickly!

By 2006, I had lived far from Murida for nearly thirty years. But emotionally, we had remained close. So in my office in Cincinnati, I asked my assistant to close the door and waited to make the call.

Over the course of my career, I've broken bad news to many a patient. I'd done it, I thought, with professionalism and empathy. But neither professionalism nor empathy would help in telling a dear sister that she had cancer. This was completely different. This time, I needed a lot of courage and some finesse.

Over the previous twenty years, I'd seen American and Arab patients react very differently to diagnoses of chronic illness or cancer. While most Americans seemed to accept their illness and immediately ask about treatment options, Arabs agonized over "why me?"—as though the disease were a punishment for something they or their ancestors had done.

As I sat in my office, I felt lucky that I was telling Murida by phone and not face to face. Over the phone, I could express false courage and might even make myself believe it. In any case, I had to do it. This was one of the many responsibilities that came with being the doctor in the family. I would do it to the best of my abilities, even though I was disappointed that no one had told me about Murida's trips to the doctor until now.

I knew my sister's fear of disease, so I was prepared to tread carefully. But, in that moment, I still had no doubt that what had happened with our nephew Waleed was wrong, and that Murida had to know the whole truth. I would not say she had a "chronic inflammation" or a "tumor" or a "touch of…." I would simply say cancer. Yes, "that disease."

Finally, I placed the call.

I like to think that I'd always been good at connecting with patients. As a medical student and intern, I often succeeded where others did not. One of my professors could not convince a man to get a lung biopsy to check for cancer, because the man feared that, if he had cancer, the biopsy would spread it. That was a common misconception at the time.

Slowly and gently, I convinced the man this wasn't true. Finally, the man agreed to the biopsy, and he appreciated knowing that his disease wasn't cancer. In exchange, the man helped fix up a car that would allow me—the boy with polio, who didn't have strength in his legs—to drive. Just as I'd helped him discover good news, he helped me achieve a dream I'd never thought would come true.

But sometimes, the news for patients was bad. As a specialist in severe skin diseases, I often had to break bad news to patients. But I had no experience in giving bad news to anyone so close as my dear sister Murida.

When I called Manal's apartment, Mona picked up the phone. She said that they'd given Murida a Xanax, telling her that she looked irritable and anxious, so that she'd be better able to handle the news. Mahmoud, his sisters, and their husbands were all there.

"Where is she?" I asked.

"She's in the living room. I'm in the bedroom. I told her that you called me yesterday as you sometimes do, and I told you about her condition."

After our hushed discussion, Mona went to the living room and handed the phone to her mother. "It's Uncle Diya. He wants to know how you are."

Murida gripped the phone. "How are you *khayya*, my dear brother?"

"I'm fine. How do you feel? Do you have any pain?"

"No, I never had any pain. I'm just waiting for the test results. I'm sick of waiting—everything takes so long."

"Mahmoud faxed me the results just now," I said, although there were no lab results.

"You have the results? Why didn't he tell me?" Murida pulled the phone away from her mouth. "Mahmoud?"

"Murida, are you there?"

"Yes."

"He just wanted me to make sure what the surgeon told him was one hundred percent accurate. And this way, I can answer any questions you might have."

"What did the surgeon say? And when did Mahmoud know?"

"He just knew. He called and faxed me the report right away."

"Oh my God, so what is it? Is it…."

"Yes it is 'the disease,' but—"

I heard Mona on the other side of the phone, calling, "Mama, Mama." I later learned that, the moment Murida heard *the disease,* she dropped the phone. As she told her children later, her body felt paralyzed. She lost control over her muscles, her mouth felt dry, and her mind went numb. Mahmoud helped push her body back into the armchair, and he sat on the left arm of the chair with his arm wrapped around her neck. Manal rushed to get Murida water in the brass cup that was kept for this sort of thing—for a sudden surprise from bad news, dizzy spells, or fainting. It was said that drinking from this cup would help a person recover from shock and even ward off the effects of the evil eye, especially if the water was from the blessed Zamzam well in Mecca.

All Mahmoud and his sisters could understand was "No way...why me...God, no....no, it's not possible." After a moment, Murida regained control of her muscles, but for the rest of the evening, she didn't utter a word. She appeared silent, shocked, and dazed, but uncomplaining. Much later, she told me that after she heard the words "the disease," a wave of fear rose up and seized her. She'd considered the possibility that she might have cancer, but now that it was a reality, she was swept away by a new force.

I remembered, then, how surprised I'd been at Muhiba's similar shock—when the doctor said my nephew Waleed had cancer. A week before, a biopsy of one of his lymph nodes had already indicated that cancer was spreading from somewhere in the belly. Still, when she heard "colon cancer," she'd frozen in disbelief.

Murida's children and their spouses chatted around her, hoping to engage my sister in small talk and take her mind off the bad news. But Murida heard nothing and thought nothing. If she did, she might have questioned God's wisdom in giving her cancer. Hadn't she suffered enough in her life? She'd just started living after getting all the girls married. Her life had just started at the age of sixty-three.

Murida could've had a different fate. Father had offered to break off her engagement to Saleem. The neighbor's son, Fawzi, had wanted to marry her, and Fawzi turned out to be a nice and successful man. It was true that Fawzi was not handsome or highly educated, but he liked Murida. He was average, but kind, and had none of Saleem's unusual manners.

But how could she have broken off the engagement? Everyone knew about it, and who would respect a previously engaged girl? So Murida went ahead with her marriage to Saleem, and moved with him into the small tin-roofed house in the camp.

Their wedding was an ordinary one: The bride and groom sat on two adjacent chairs in a living room that had been emptied of furniture and stacked with small chairs rented for the occasion. A small space in front of the bride and groom was left for dancers: old school friends of the bride, as well as women and girls from both families. It was her friends' duty to dance, and those who were closer were expected to dance more rounds, accompanied by clapping from those who were watching. Before invitation cards became the norm, family members went to peoples' homes to invite them, and kids gathered at the windows to watch and get candy or a sweet drink.

CHAPTER TWELVE

Once my sister was back home from Manal's, and she was in her bedroom, she performed her last prayer of the day: the fifth. She'd long ago memorized each of the prayers, and could do them while half-asleep. But this time, her mind and spirit weren't in it. She couldn't erase the idea of her cancer, not for a second. Even when she would drift off a little, the first thing that came to mind when she woke up was *cancer*. The name didn't matter any longer—it could be "the disease" or "cancer." She has a thing inside her that was evil, destructive, and merciless. If she could, she'd dig it out with her own hands. Yes, she had enough strength to do that.

How could this alien life be inside of her body, eating away at it, growing at her expense? Her body no longer belonged to her alone: She shared it with another creature. What kind of disease was this? No wonder people feared it. Although she prayed, she didn't ask God for help. Suddenly, she stopped believing in miracles.

Am I angry with God? Murida paused. She didn't dare accept the idea of being mad at God—she believed in Him, and she needed Him. Yet she did not understand His actions towards her. He could have made it benign. Why hadn't He? Doesn't the Quran say "He is capable of doing all things"?

No, Murida wasn't really angry, just feeling sorry for herself as never before. All obstacles in her life until now amount to very little compared to this. Suddenly, growing up in a refugee camp, having girls, marrying Saleem, and never having enough income were minor annoyances, not worthy of her attention.

Still, how could this be? She'd invested her faith in a just God, because that's what she'd read in the Quran and what Muslim scholars said on TV and the radio. Throughout her life, she'd depended only on herself and God. She believed that God answered good people's prayers and rewarded those who suffered. It was true that some rewards happened after death, but Murida wished to collect her reward during her lifetime.

Surely, Murida thought, God had been watching as she'd struggled to feed a family of nine with just one kilo of meat in her stew. She'd told the kids to take big bites of bread with each mouthful so that the meal would stretch to feed all nine people.

All the children knew that their father didn't make much money and that they couldn't eat rich food regularly. They wore their clothes until they were too small, and dresses moved down from older sister to younger. Still, no one complained.

Murida always felt terrible that they couldn't afford enough meat. She believed that the children couldn't stay healthy eating only vegetables and legumes. But what could she do? She couldn't tell Saleem to work more—he wasn't capable of it. His pace was slow. He called it *meticulous*. But, whether meticulous or slow, he was paid for the work he completed, not a fixed salary.

Saleem often went for weeks without work, yet he never apologized. He'd retired soon after turning fifty, soon after Mahmoud had graduated and started working. And while he knew that Murida was making money off her sewing, he never thanked her for the additional income. He never even acknowledged her work.

Well, Saleem did acknowledge it every now and again, when he would yell at her for working instead of looking after his needs, such as making him tea or a meal. She would say "in a few minutes," and he would shout, "You always say 'in a few minutes.' I'm sick of this machine. One day, I'm going to throw it off the balcony." After that, Murida would always stop working.

That evening, as Murida prayed, Saleem sat in the other room watching TV. After she finished, Murida returned to the living room and told her husband that she was going to bed.

Saleem looked up momentarily from the TV. "Cheer up, you'll be fine."

Murida had no answer to this, and she went back to the bedroom, looking gloomy. This irritated Saleem, who turned off the television and followed her into the bedroom.

"What's going on?" Saleem asked. "Didn't Mahmoud say that the doctor took it all out? Why are you still upset?" Murida had no intention of responding. If he couldn't understand what she was going through, then there was no use in saying anything.

In order to avoid a lecture, Murida nodded. "I'm okay, just tired." Fortunately, after this, he left her alone.

The next morning, as Murida talked with her eldest daughter Maha, she felt more and more certain that the matter wasn't finished. It was cancer, after all, and Murida needed to see another doctor, a cancer specialist, in order to understand what to do. The doctor who operated on her was not a specialist in cancer treatment—he was only a surgeon. She'd heard people talk about chemotherapy: Would she need it? So she called Mahmoud, who was fortunate to get an appointment for the following day in the recently opened cancer division at the new Dubai Hospital.

Again, Mona drove her mother to the appointment, but this time Ghina and Amal also went along. This time, the place was brand new and the cancer specialist was a gentle young Sudanese man sitting behind a fancy desk. While Murida and Mona sat across from the doctor, he reviewed the materials that they'd given him, including the pathology report on the lump and the previous year's blood-test results. The Sudanese doctor had Murida go into the adjacent examining room and take off her shirt so that he could make his own examination of her breasts. The short exam surprised Murida. The doctor spent more time feeling under her left arm than he did her breast. Then, after just a minute or two, he returned to his desk. Mona and Murida took their seats opposite the doctor.

"I'm sorry to tell you that the pathology report doesn't show that all of the cancerous tissue was removed. It's very possible that there's more cancerous tissue still in the breast."

"But the surgeon said—"

Before Mona could finish, the doctor interrupted. "The cancer is present around the edges of the specimen, which means there is still cancer in the breast. And the lymph nodes feel large to me."

Murida took in a deep breath. *Oh my God, what a liar that surgeon was.*

"What does that mean?" Mona asked.

"It means the cancer may have spread to the nearby lymph nodes."

Murida almost fainted. She felt she was in another world.

"So what do we do next?" Ghina asked.

"Before any decision is made, you need a lot more tests, mostly x-rays. At the very least, you'll need a mastectomy, which means removing the whole breast, as well as lymph nodes to check for the cancer's spread. This is to check on the extent of any remaining cancer."

"Will you do that?" Mona asked.

"No, I'm not a surgeon. After that, we'll decide if you need chemo, radiation, or hormones, which I can do."

Mona nodded.

"But these are very expensive treatments and tests. Do you have a government card?"

"We're not Emirati," Mona said. "We're from Palestine."

"Ah," the doctor said. "I'm sorry for what happened to your country. We need to get Jerusalem back to the Muslims."

"Thank you. So what do you suggest?"

"The tests, the surgery, and all the treatments will cost tens of thousands of dollars. If you know anyone at Twam cancer hospital in Al-Ain, then have them help you to get in there. It's an excellent hospital that has modern facilities and is qualified by the Americans. And there, you won't have to pay. It's free."

Fortunately, Mona already had a plan.

One thing Murida had felt lucky about, after moving to Dubai, was the free education for her children. In Lebanon, we Palestinians attended special public schools that didn't prepare us to pass the difficult French-style Baccalaureate exams required for university admission. If Murida had stayed in Lebanon, she would've had to pay for private high schools as well as university for each of her children, which would've been impossible. Our father worked very hard to send most of his children to expensive private high schools. In Dubai, all of Murida's children were able to finish high school for free. The eldest three even attended university for free. At that time, it was available to non-citizens, and they had such high marks in high school that they were welcomed with open arms.

When it came time for Manal to go to university, the rules had changed, and public universities were limited to Emiratis only. So the rest of the children got their degrees from a distance university in Beirut. After finishing high school, each of the last four girls worked as a secretary or typist during the day and studied at night.

Even Murida got a certificate in secretarial work, although she never worked as a typist.

Health care was also initially free for expatriates in the Emirates, although by the time Murida grew ill, they had to pay. She had no idea how to pay for expensive cancer treatments.

On the way back to Murida's apartment, Murida turned to her daughter. "Do we know anyone who can speak for us, so that I could go to Al-Ain?"

"Rana."

"Mahmoud's wife?"

"She already told me yesterday that, if you needed to go to Twam, her friend is the director's personal assistant. Rana said that the director respects her friend a lot and treats her like a daughter."

"Oh God, please call her."

Mona smiled as best she could. "I'll call at five, when she's back home from school. I think Sheikh Zayed made it for everyone in the UAE, not just citizens. But right now, can we go get coffee somewhere?"

"As you wish, *habibti*, may God keep you for me and for your family."

As they drove, Mona felt saddened by the certainty with which the doctor had talked about residual cancer. For the past thirty-six hours, Mona had believed that her mother was cancer-free, at least for the time being. That's what the surgeon had told Mahmoud. Now, a specialist was saying otherwise. He seemed honest and knowledgeable—there was little reason to doubt him. Of course everything, in the end, was in God's hands. He was the decider.

But, as she drove, Mona began preparing herself for the worst. She had to read more and ask questions. She would have to understand the reasons behind each of the doctors' decisions, and she would have to be honest with her mother. Murida had to know everything along the way. They couldn't let her be caught unawares like she was two days ago. They had to face this with their eyes open.

At the Starbucks where she and Mona stopped for drinks, Murida saw only young, healthy-looking people. They looked so different from how Murida had been in her youth. They wore Western clothes—blouses and jeans—and boys and girls mixed freely, with fancy mobile phones and their own cars. The girl's blouses were tiny and one could see the skin of their abdomen, even their navels. Murida felt it really wasn't proper, not healthy, to expose one's body that way.

But these young people had already done so much more than her. Murida had had so few experiences! For the first eighteen years of her life, she'd rarely done anything that could be considered fun. She never left home except to take the dough to the neighborhood oven or to carry water to fill the reservoir that sat on top of the kitchen. Or she would go to school, or buy something for her mother from the local grocery shop. She had just a few friends from school that she might see accidentally while doing chores. Even on the Eid, she rarely did anything that could be seen as fun or entertainment. She watched her two young brothers, me and Mutasim, get dressed up and go out with pocket money, while she stayed home.

Since Murida had gotten married, she'd been to the movie theater only twice. She *loved* the movies. They told the stories that she didn't have time to read in books. Fortunately, they ultimately showed most films on TV. Movies and TV dramas transported Murida to a fantasy place for an hour or two, offering a much-needed break from her daily routine. In the coming months, Murida would need this chance to escape more and more.

After their drinks, Mona took her mother home and went back to her own apartment. When five o'clock came around, Mona went into her bedroom, closed the door, and called Rana. As she explained everything to her sister-in-law, she spoke in a quiet voice, as if she were afraid of letting the cancer genie out of its bottle.

"So can you talk to Samira tonight?" Mona asked.

"I'll call her now. She leaves work around six o'clock, and, if I call now, I can catch her before her boss leaves. But I think they'll take Murida. I'll call you back soon."

While she waited, Mona called her mother. "Rana is calling her friend Samira right now. After that, she'll call us."

Murida held the phone tightly. "Who would've thought my fate would be in the hands of Mahmoud's wife? So many good things have come to me through my only son, God bless him."

It wasn't long before Rana called back. Unfortunately, she told Mona, the hospital director was on a trip and would be away for the next two days. But, she added, Samira was certain that they would take Murida as a patient. It was only a matter of having an empty bed.

Hearing this, Murida felt almost happy. If Murida was accepted into Twam hospital, then her son wouldn't have to spend tens of thousands of dollars on her care. She would feel terrible if he had to spend that much money on her medical bills. After all, Mahmoud had a family to care for and three boys to educate. He would need a lot of money to get three boys through private schools and, later, college. *Nothing that I've done for my son would justify draining his savings for my illness.* She would rather go to a cheap hospital and hope for the best, even though getting inexpensive medical care in the Emirates was fraught with risks. Public hospitals weren't as good, and private hospitals were very expensive.

For the next few days, Murida hoped that she had found a solution.

I wasn't the only one who learned about Murida's cancer in those days. Murida's children also decided to tell our other siblings. So, as Murida waited to hear about Twam hospital, our two sisters who lived in the Emirates—Ilham and Suad—filled her with stories about unreliable Emirati hospitals.

Ilham and Suad hadn't been to see Murida in a long time, as their lives had grown apart. First, Murida had moved to Dubai in 1977. The next year, Suad married and moved to Abu Dhabi, and four years later, in 1982, Ilham and her family moved from Libya to Sharjah. Although they weren't far away, each had their own life to live. For many years, they saw each other just once or twice a year, on holy days. Ilham had five children to care for and worked as a teacher. Murida was busy raising seven children, while Suad was finding her way through a lonely life as she dealt with episodes of depression and anxiety, homesickness, and marital problems.

Suad and Ilham also felt that Murida prized her children so highly that there was no room for affection towards them. Murida, meanwhile, thought her two more educated sisters thought little of her. Probably none of them was right, for when they all met, they laughed like young innocents. Ilham and Suad respected what Murida had accomplished with her children, in spite of her husband. None of the three sisters would ever admit to feeling jealous of the other two. But, since our mother had taught her children to compete with one another, it was likely that they all experienced some amount of jealousy.

When they learned that Murida had fallen sick, Suad and Ilham were shocked. They were shocked that their less-fortunate sister had developed such a serious disease, but also that cancer had come so close to them. They began visiting Murida on the day after my call from America. They both insisted that the hospitals in the Emirates weren't good and often made mistakes. They told her that, for example, they knew a woman who was told she had cancer at an Emirati hospital. But after going to the AUB hospital in Beirut, the woman found that all she had was a benign tumor!

Ilham and Suad believed that Murida didn't really have cancer. Despite their nephew Waleed's early death, they still felt there was no cancer among the

Mutasims. But if Murida had cancer, they thought, then the whole family was at risk. Once cancer entered a family, no one knew who was next.

CHAPTER THIRTEEN

Murida was at her youngest daughter's apartment when she got a call from Rana, telling her that she could go to Twam Hospital as early as the next day. They had a bed available.

Murida was happy. She was happy for several reasons, chief among them that she would be able to stay at one hospital rather than traipsing from one place to another. All that she might need was available at Twam. She didn't mind the idea of staying a few days at the hospital, although she hated being bedbound.

Twam Hospital was in Al-Ain, two hours away from Dubai, Sharjah, and Abu Dhabi. But the next morning, Mahmoud, Mona, and Ghina all rode along to the hospital with Murida and Saleem. The mood in the car wasn't gloomy. They were all open to the unknown, and none of them thought the cancer had spread to other organs. Unlike on previous car rides, this time they all talked about many things: how great Rana was, how disciplined her three boys were, how lucky the grandchildren were, all excelling in school. They also discussed where they would stay in Al-Ain during Murida's time in the hospital. The one thing they didn't talk about was cancer.

The admissions procedures took less than an hour, and Murida was in a room by noon. They drew blood from her, placing it in tubes of different sizes and colors. Looking at how much blood they took, Murida wondered if she would become anemic, but the technician assured her that she would be fine. They brought a meal that wasn't bad by hospital standards: a leg of chicken, mixed vegetables, rice, tea, and a piece of cake. Murida ate it all, and Mahmoud went to get sandwiches from the coffee shop for everyone else. He walked back into the room and set down a variety of cold sandwiches: some with cheese, some with labneh and sliced cucumber, and some with turkey.

"Is that all they had?" Saleem asked.

Ghina seemed annoyed. "What did you expect?"

"At least a hot sandwich with meat"

Ghina stared at her father. "They don't have shawarma, it's a hospital."

"Fine, fine, I should've kept my mouth shut."

The others said nothing, fearing that the argument would escalate. The daughters made eye contact with one another. The girls always felt more irritated by their father's behavior than Mahmoud did.

Mahmoud was more sympathetic to Saleem than his sisters were. He felt that his father was unfortunate, as he hadn't had a father of his own. Saleem's father had died before he was born and his mother blamed Saleem for being a bad omen. In response, she neglected him, and Saleem was raised by his older sisters.

As an adult, Mahmoud often found excuses for his father's behaviors. On the rare occasion when Murida complained to Mahmoud about something that his father had done to her, Mahmoud usually suggested that she might've said or done something to aggravate him. For a long time, Murida didn't understand why. Everyone else took her side, so why not her only son?

Murida couldn't remember exactly when Mahmoud had started taking his father's side. She knew that the father and son weren't close during Mahmoud's childhood, so perhaps it was when Mahmoud finished university and was looking for a bride. Whenever it had happened, she thought, it was good. It was better for Mahmoud to believe that his father deserved respect.

Over the next two days, Murida took three separate trips to the radiology unit for various tests. In between tests, she grew bored. They still weren't telling her anything, and she spent most of her day in bed. The nurses expected her to stay in bed, and Murida wanted to follow their orders. She felt lucky to be at Twam Hospital, and she wanted to be on very good terms with the nurses. She wanted them to like her so that they would give her the best possible care. All of the nurses were non-Arab—mostly Filipino and Malaysian—but they spoke enough Arabic to communicate with patients.

In the mornings, a team of doctors and nurses stopped by Murida's room. Each time, Murida asked about test results, but the doctors had no answers. They were waiting for the reports, they said. On the third day, a doctor assured her that the blood tests, done on samples taken the first day, were all normal.

"That's good news, isn't it?" Murida asked.

"Yes," the doctor said. "But we still need to wait for the other tests before we can decide what to do next."

"What are you looking for?"

"We want to make sure the cancer is limited to the breast and hasn't spread anywhere else."

"When will you know?"

"I hope tomorrow."

Murida sat up in the bed. "Should I ask my son to be here?"

"Yes."

Murida appreciated the doctor's gentle nature. He had a thin beard, and spoke softly and wasn't bossy. He also seemed to respect the fact that she was a woman, unlike the Lebanese surgeon. Mona had learned from one of the nurses that this was the chemo doctor.

The chemo doctor had a wedding band, Murida noticed, so he must be married. *God protect him for his family.*

After the visit, Murida called Mahmoud, asking him to be there in the morning. Mahmoud was worried that, even if he left first thing in the morning, he might not arrive in time to meet with the doctors. He thought for a moment and told his mother that Amal's family driver would pick up Mona and Ghina that evening and drive them up to al-Ain. That way, they would definitely be with her in the morning.

Mahmoud called Mona and Ghina, and they agreed that they would stay at the furnished apartment that the family had rented in al-Ain, where their father had been sleeping for the past few days. Mahmoud reassured Murida that he would leave home by 6:30 a.m. and, in all likelihood, he'd be there before the doctors did their rounds.

Murida set down the phone, feeling reassured. She didn't want it to be just her and Saleem when she got the news. If it was good news, she wanted to celebrate with as many of her children as possible. If it was bad news, she would hate to be alone in the room with Saleem.

If Murida's body was clear, she thought then she'd have a second chance at life! After this, she promised herself that she would live every day to its fullest. She would find ways to enjoy each and every moment, and she wouldn't allow herself to be hurt or even bothered by Saleem. She'd given him forty-five years of her life—the rest would be hers. She'd earned it.

Murida vowed that she wouldn't be mean, but she'd either stand up to Saleem or write him off. He wouldn't control her life any more. After this, she would eat better food and worry less about money. Mahmoud would provide for them. Besides, she'd saved up $15,000 from a combination of work, the monthly allowance that Mahmoud gave them, and the cash that her daughters had given her on Mother's Day and other occasions.

Of course, Saleem didn't know about this little stash—the money was held in a joint account with Mona. Murida wondered what he would say about it if he knew. It surely wouldn't be good.

If she was cancer-free, Murida thought, she would visit her mother in Beirut every year. She wished that her father were still alive, as she had dearly loved and respected him. She loved our mother, too, but she didn't look up to Mother as she'd looked up to Father. Murida thought our mother was selfish and gossipy, while our father had been a hard-working gentleman.

Well, our father was a gentleman except for one thing: Murida had seen him verbally attack our mother in public. Our father was Murida's hero in every way except for how he verbally abused our mother. Murida could never reconcile his two personalities, but it did help her survive life with Saleem. If Father could be mean and abusive, then Saleem could not be blamed. After all, he was less than our father.

If Murida got better, she thought that she would definitely take long visits to Beirut, perhaps two or three months at a time. She and Saleem owned an apartment in Beirut now—Mahmoud had bought it for them two years ago. From there, it was just a five-minute walk to our parents' home, and it wasn't much farther to see two aunts, two uncles, and Muhiba. She would visit Mother every day and stop by our uncle's apartment in the same building. After that, she would either go to an aunt or to Muhiba.

Murida promised herself that she would try to be better friends with her oldest sister. She would be more forgiving of Muhiba's behavior—yes, she would disarm her tough older sister with kindness. If she and Muhiba were closer, perhaps Muhiba would treat Ghina with more respect, and maybe even with a little love. After all, Ghina's children were Muhiba's grandchildren.

Everyone knew that Muhiba and her husband didn't approve of their son's marriage to Murida's youngest. They'd made it as clear as possible for such a sensitive topic. They felt very strongly that their dear architect son had made a poor choice. Many a good girl would've been happy to marry Khaled, yet he chose the daughter of Saleem and Murida. In doing so, Khaled had married down, and his parents felt a man should marry someone of his own social standing.

It had been terribly obvious during Ghina and Khaled's small engagement party that Muhiba and her husband didn't approve of Murida's daughter. Neither of them had even bothered to fake a smile. It had been horrible for Murida, and Ghina had felt so badly that she'd come home that night and asked her mother to annul the engagement. Some people had already told Murida that her sister was badmouthing Ghina—but Murida had decided that was not going to get in the way of Ghina's marriage.

No way, Murida had said, even though she'd witnessed the ill-treatment herself. She told her daughter to be patient, to remember that she wouldn't be living in the same country as her future in-laws. Murida told Ghina that Khaled loved her, and he wouldn't be living under his mother's thumb. Soon, they would all go back to Dubai, and Ghina wouldn't see her Beiruti in-laws for at least another year, until the following summer. When they were in Dubai, Murida promised, Khaled would take Ghina places and get her presents.

He was a genuinely kind and gentle young man, and would treat Ghina just like his father treated his mother, with the utmost love and respect.

Ghina took her mother's advice and went ahead with the marriage. She'd wanted to finish university, but once she decided to get married, that put an end to the idea of a college degree. Ghina was as academically accomplished as Mona, and she could've gotten a degree with ease. Still, Murida thought, a girl needed a husband more than a degree. She would hardly ever use her degree once she became a mother. Being a proper mother was a full-time job. At least, Murida said, it was if you didn't ask foreign maids to raise your child, as many middle-class women did all over the Gulf countries.

Murida knew that Ghina was her most strong-willed daughter. Ghina didn't accept any abuse, and she told things as she saw them. Still, Ghina was not able to hold her own against Muhiba, who was much older and more experienced in the ways of arguments.

The night before Murida was to hear from the doctors, Ghina and Mona arrived at nine p.m. and were happy to find their mother in a good mood. They thought she must have finally accepted her fate.

The two sisters had to track down their father to explain why they had come to Twam so late at night and to tell him about the doctor's planned visit. Saleem had already found ways to keep busy. He did his five prayers, made a few visits to the coffee shop on the first floor, and visited the male patient wing, chatting with whoever was willing. He'd also discovered the nurses' break room, where he would get biscuits and make hot tea. He took his own breaks in the evening, when the temperature went down, and walked around the hospital grounds among the palm trees. There, he made calls to people he knew in Sharjah and Dubai. Saleem loved his cell phone, and hardly ever parted with it. He often held it in his hand while walking, even when he wasn't using it.

It was around 8:30 the next morning when the doctor and his team stopped by Murida's room. Mona offered the doctor the chair she was sitting on, and he sat down while the rest of his team stood behind him or beside him.

The doctor asked Murida how she felt.

"I feel good. What did the tests show?"

"Well," the doctor said, "your blood tests are all good. The total body scan showed that your internal organs are all normal, your chest x-ray is normal, and the bone scan is normal. That's generally where we worry the breast cancer may spread to."

"Thank you doctor, and thank God," Murida said.

Ghina was wondering silently: *But what about the breast test, the mammogram?*

The doctor nodded, seeming to read her mind. "The mammogram showed you still have some cancerous tissue."

"The Dubai surgeon told my son that he took it all out."

The doctor leaned forward, his expression gentle but serious. "He must have taken the main lump, the primary tumor, which is where the cancer started. But it seems that it also spread into a few smaller lumps that the doctor couldn't feel by hand, because they are too small."

"But the mammogram I did in Dubai didn't show other lumps."

"I can't comment on that without seeing it, but we have the newest equipment in the world here, maybe that's why."

"So how do we get rid of them, the small lumps? Cut them out?"

"No, we have to take out the whole breast."

Murida remained silent.

"We also have to remove some tissue from your armpit and test it to see if the cancer has spread to your lymph nodes. Then we'll be able to decide about chemo, radiation, and other treatments."

Murida choked back her sadness and frustration. Even though she tried to hold it in, tears rolled down her cheeks to her chin. Ghina wiped them with a tissue while holding back her own tears.

"I talked to the surgeon, and he can operate the day after tomorrow in the morning," the doctor said. "Unless you want to go home for few days first"

Murida shook her head.

"Then I'll stop back later today, before I leave, and check to see if you need anything or have other questions. Okay?"

Mona and Ghina both thanked the doctor, while Saleem stayed quiet until the team left the room.

"You'll be okay," Saleem said to Murida. "Remember what's-her-name—they removed her breast and she's still strong twenty years later. God will help you."

Ghina asked her father to go get them tea. He shrugged and strolled out and down the hallway. Murida seemed to be in deep thought, so Ghina asked what she was thinking about.

"Nothing" Murida said. "What will be, will be. I thought right from the beginning that, if it was cancer, they might need to remove the whole breast."

Mona moved closer to her mother. "That's what God has planned for you. He has a plan for each of us."

"I never imagined that I'd lose a breast. I remember when they removed that woman's breast—I felt so sorry for her. But she's fine now and doesn't even try to hide it. I wish I could be like her."

"You will be, God willing." Mona picked up a cup that her father had left on the window sill. "Can I get you something to drink or eat? I saw that you left your breakfast tray almost untouched."

"I have no appetite."

"Let me get you some fresh mango juice," Ghina said. "There's a man just outside the hospital, and I can pick the mangoes myself. He looks clean. He also has ripe guava, so I can get you guava juice, too."

"Just guava please," Murida said in a small voice.

Ghina gave her mother a last look before she left the room.

Murida turned to the other side of the bed, where Mona sat on a chair. "What do you think *habibti*?"

"About what?"

"The surgery."

"You don't have a choice, so don't think about it. I hear it's become simple, as it's been done on so many women."

"I know."

"Do you want to go out? It's not too hot today. We can sit on a bench and have the juice."

"As you wish, may God bless you."

Although they were all optimistic about the surgery, Mona felt that her mother should enjoy life in the moments she could. At sixty-three years old, that was perhaps Murida's most important job. And she had one other important job: to repair one of her oldest relationships.

For as long as Murida could remember, she and my sister Muhiba had had a difficult relationship. Murida had long known that Muhiba didn't approve of their children even playing together, but Ghina and Khaled had nonetheless found love.

Yet a few years after they were married, Ghina was still fighting for her in-laws' respect. After many years, she finally gave up and stopped caring for her mother-in-law's approval. Murida was upset about it, yet never dared raise the issue with her older sister, assuming that Muhiba would deny it, or would blame Ghina and mention her "lack of social class," which would risk setting off a fight that we were all sure to regret.

Murida was never entirely sure why the two hadn't gotten along. Perhaps it was because Muhiba had been jealous that her younger sister had studied through the sixth grade, while Muhiba had stopped at first. Muhiba could barely read and couldn't write a letter, while Murida wrote good letters to her parents. Perhaps it was because Muhiba had to work in the candy factory while her sister went to school. Perhaps it was because Muhiba thought she was the pretty one in the family, or that she was smarter, classier, and shrewder. Maybe it was because her husband was superior to Saleem in every way.

Sometimes, Murida felt that she must be the inferior one—why else would our parents have offered her

Saleem as a potential husband? Murida admitted that part of the problem was her jealousy: She was jealous of Muhiba having three sons and a better husband, and this was part of the undeclared tension. Also, Muhiba's husband didn't care for Murida's husband, and he let it be known whenever the two were together in public, even though the two were first cousins.

Muhiba's husband mocked Saleem and laughed cynically at his comments. Murida wanted Saleem to defend himself, but he was either clueless or unable to defend himself against such a smooth talker. So Murida had to defend her husband by confronting Muhiba's husband. She knew that when she did so, she appeared snappish and aggressive, but she couldn't remain silent while her man was being insulted.

Finally, at the end of June 2006, it was time for Murida's mastectomy. All of her children—except Hanan, who had just immigrated to Canada— were there. They arrived the night before and slept together at the rented apartment. The women had to share beds, just as they had when they were girls. Of all of them, Maha was the most anxious. She saw her mother less often, and on that night she spoke freely about her worries. Ghina told her to stop worrying or at least to stop talking about it. Mahmoud, Mona, and Ghina had taken on leadership roles in the group, but even those who seemed strong were tense.

Manal was sitting on one of the beds. "Do you think Mother will be okay?"

Mona, who was lying beside her, gave a firm nod. "I'm sure of it. She's strong, and this is the best hospital in the Emirates. All we can hope for is that God keeps an eye on her."

By then, Mona had been observant for five years, and always wore a headscarf when she was outside or in the company of men. Mona's daughter Tala had followed in her mother's footsteps and also wore a scarf. Throughout her mother's illness, Mona's faith kept growing, and years later, when she would move to Canada with her children, she would continue to read the Quran and other Islamic literature daily.

The sisters had barely fallen asleep when the alarm clock woke them at 6:30 a.m. They wanted to get to the hospital and spend some time with their mother before she was taken into surgery, so they dressed quickly and arrived in the room around an hour later.

By that time, Murida was awake and eager to go. That's how she was: Once a decision had been made, there was no reason to hesitate, no matter how daunting or difficult the road ahead. In this, Murida was like our father. Mother had been the opposite, and Murida was glad she didn't resemble her. Murida wanted that "monster" out of her body, every last cell of it. If she had to sacrifice her breast, so be it. Indeed, she had come to hate her sick breast. For the past few days, she'd avoided touching it or looking at it in the mirror. She'd convinced herself that she wanted nothing more than to see it gone.

The night before Murida's mastectomy, a social worker had visited in order to help Murida deal with the loss of her breast. Among other things, the young woman asked Murida how she thought her husband would deal with her the loss of her breast, and how it would affect their physical intimacy. Murida was embarrassed by the question.

"He's old and we don't worry about these things" was all that Murida could say. After the social worker left, Murida thought she would give up both breasts if it meant she would be cured.

Murida's younger sisters Suad and Ilham also knew about the mastectomy, and they arrived at the hospital around ten a.m. Suad had just returned from a few years' stay in Lebanon, where she'd gone to care for her children, who were studying at the American University in Beirut.

The day before, Ilham had learned from Amal about the extent of Murida's cancer, and she'd gone right over to tell Suad. As soon as Suad opened the door, she knew from the ashen look on her sister's face that it must be bad news. Before Ilham could say a word, Suad clapped a hand against her mouth and began to cry. Suad had suffered her own share of miseries and cried easily at bad news, especially news about health. As a child, Suad had suffered from a kidney disorder that caused her severe back pain and required hospitalization and many months of cortisone treatments. The process had changed her physical appearance dramatically and had also encouraged her hypochondriac tendencies. Like our mother, she became afraid of disease, or any symptoms that she could not easily explain.

In the last two hours before surgery, Murida was in the company of all her children save one, as well as two of her sisters, her aunt, and Saleem. She felt loved and cherished, emotions that she had experienced only too rarely. Why did it take cancer for people to show her their love? Well, Murida thought, it was probably always like that: People assumed that they'd live forever and forgot to do good until moments like this, when they feared losing someone. Murida wondered: *Was this how all people were? Or was it just Palestinians, who had been forced to suppress their feelings in order to survive?*

At eleven a.m., an orderly and a nurse came to take Murida to the operating room. At last, she thought, they would take the monster out. Yet she had tears in her eyes. What if something went wrong during several hours of surgery? She recalled how, when she was ten or eleven, her maternal grandfather, who hadn't even been sixty, had gone in to have simple eye surgery. He'd "never woken up," and our mother had been devastated. They said he died soon after they gave him the shot of anesthesia. Could Murida have a similar destiny?

As Murida was being wheeled down the hallway to surgery, everyone except our aunt with arthritis walked alongside the gurney. Everyone—even Ilham and Suad—gazed at her with eyes full of affection before she disappeared. Murida had never before allowed herself to think that they really loved her.

But the real surprise was that Saleem was crying for the first time since Murida's illness had been diagnosed. Everyone was crying, but Saleem's cry was different. It was the cry of an abandoned child. He was wailing and didn't seem to try to control himself or to attempt to support his children—it was as though he were the only one walking along with Murida.

What if his wife didn't come back? Patients had been known to die on the operating table. Could she be among them? She would be leaving him, just as his parents had. Did he realize, in that moment, that he'd been treating Murida as though she were the mother who'd abandoned him? Probably not.

Suad and Ilham, who knew how Saleem acted around their sister, were shocked at his wailing. They thought that he was realizing, for the first time, that he wouldn't be complete without her, just as he hadn't been complete without a mother and father.

In the coffee shop, the rest of the family talked about their hopes for Murida's future, dwelling on examples of two women who were still doing well ten and twenty years after mastectomies. The family felt optimistic, and why not? Tests showed that all the organs were clear. The conversation buoyed their moods, and they found themselves able to laugh for the first time in days. Suad acted silly in order to help them laugh, and to take her fragile mind off of events. Only Mahmoud wouldn't laugh. He couldn't take his mind off the seriousness of the situation. His mother was being cut, and they laughed. Still, he understood, and he left his aunts and sisters to their laughter. At the time for the noon prayer, Mahmoud called his father's cell phone, and they both went to clear their minds and pray.

Five hours after she was taken in, God answered their prayers. Murida's daughters were gathered in Murida's room when a nurse came in and told them she just received a phone call from the recovery room: Murida Mutasim was fine. Everyone thanked her profusely for the good news. Mahmoud could barely contain his emotions, and had to leave to hide his tears. All he could whisper to himself was, "Thank you, God."

CHAPTER FOURTEEN

It was three days after the surgery when I arrived at the Dubai airport. It had been two long years since I'd been in the Emirates, and as many years since I'd seen my older sister. My flight landed around one in the morning, and Mona drove to the airport to pick me up. Among all of Murida's children, Mona was the closest to me. Together with Tala, we made the two-hour drive back to the apartment near Twam hospital, slept a few hours, and woke at eight in the morning.

That morning, when we arrived at Twam, I admit I was curious to see how an Emirati hospital worked. I'd worked at hospitals in Lebanon and in the US, but I had no experience with Emirati healthcare. I was perhaps the first member of the family to really look at the three-story building, which was surrounded by rows of short palm trees. Each was bright green and well-groomed, surrounded by flowering shrubs and a short concrete wall to contain dirt and flowers and hold in the water.

Some of the palms had yellow or deep-red fruit, and I had a sudden craving for dates. When Murida and I had lived in the refugee camp outside Beirut, there had been a palm tree across the street from our home, on the property of a loud, mean Lebanese man. But we'd never had access to its fruit. After Murida got married and Father built two rooms on the second floor, my brother Mutasim would throw rocks at the fruit clusters from his room upstairs. Sometimes, the fruit would fall, but Mutasim didn't dare go collect it for fear of getting caught by the owner, who hated Palestinian kids. Sometimes, I would crawl under the tree and get a few dates.

Forty-some years later, we were all scattered around the world.

By this time, I'd been working in hospitals in Beirut and the U.S. for thirty years. The journey from surviving polio to chairing a department in an Ohio university hospital hadn't been an easy one. But it was also a journey that I hadn't taken alone—everyone in the family had taken it with me. They'd cheered me on, given me moral support, and prayed for me. They'd trusted my intelligence even when I didn't feel smart. They'd trusted me when I struggled with the effects of polio, and they'd still trusted me when I struggled with anxiety, depression, and low self-esteem. They elevated me in their eyes, and, against many odds, I'd succeeded. It was their faith in me—in part, Murida's faith—that had made me a doctor. Now, I felt, it was payback time.

As I approached Murida's room, I was pulled between warring emotions. I felt the anxious anticipation of seeing my strong sister in a vulnerable state, but also the pride at being the family doctor coming in to help. I could speak the doctors' language and put everyone's minds at ease. But I knew that, to do this, I had to suppress my own gloom. Whatever the result of the pathology tests, I had to appear optimistic and keep Murida's spirits high. That was my mission.

I felt sure I'd be up to the job. I had to be. I took a deep breath at the door to Murida's room, put on my characteristic wide smile, and walked in with Mona behind me. It wasn't a fake smile—I'd just put myself in the right mood, like actors do. I noticed a few people sitting around the room, but I didn't register any face except Murida's. She was propped up, halfway between sitting and lying down, but fully awake. As I walked towards the left side of the bed, Murida's expression grew concerned. She was happy to see me, I was sure. But she couldn't smile to express it.

"*Khayya* Diya, *habibi*, you came for me."

"Of course"

I set my crutch beside the bed and hugged my sister with both arms. While in America, I'd learned to hug instead of giving a kiss on the cheeks, as we'd done when I was growing up. I thought that a hug delivered more emotional weight, and, moreover, it was less contagious than kissing! My head rested against Murida's right shoulder, and she patted me on the back with her good right arm. Her left arm was swollen and painful after the removal of most of the tissue in her left armpit, which the surgeon had taken out to check for cancer in her lymph nodes.

"How do you feel?"

"They took my breast." Murida paused, choking on the sentence. "That was fine, I was prepared for that, but why did they cut open my armpit?"

"They need to check the lymph nodes. They don't want to risk leaving any cancerous cells behind."

"I have 33 sutures. I almost fainted when the nurse changed the dressing this morning. It's like a zipper."

"You'll be fine," I said. "It's better to take more than less."

"So do you think this is it?"

"I think so. But you may need chemo to be safe."

"They told me about that—and radiation." Murida paused, looking off behind me, appearing suddenly pitiful. "What did I do to get this?"

"You didn't do anything. It's just luck, bad luck."

Murida looked back at me. "Didn't I have enough bad luck in my life? I've been working since I was twelve. Now that I'm finally done, and starting to live, I get this?"

"It's not fair, I know, but you'll be okay."

"Why me of all my sisters? I had the worst luck of them all, and then this?"

"Say *alhamdulillah* and don't doubt God's wisdom," Mona said, from the side of the room. "There's a reason for everything, and we can't know it. God works in ways we don't always understand. Keep your faith in Him high."

"*Alhamdulillah*," Murida said.

After that, I turned and faced the others in the room, greeting Ghina and Amal, who'd spent the previous night with their mother and looked tired. I had already met Saleem at the apartment, and had tried to avoid a conversation with him without success. Saleem talked about the torture that Murida had been through in the previous months and how she didn't deserve this, but that "we" accept God's will, because what other choice did we have? He asked about my trip, my wife, and my sons. Saleem wanted to know: Do your boys play sports like Mahmoud's three boys, who are great at football?

I sat down beside Murida and asked Saleem to get me a hot tea. Saleem was glad to oblige and offered to bring two cups, "since they're small."

On the first evening at Twam, I had a disappointing moment, after my sister Suad told me why the surgeon was optimistic.

"I was with Mona and Mahmoud when he said that, since Murida is older, her body doesn't renew its cells as fast as if she were young," Suad said. "So the cancer cells won't regenerate and divide as quickly. He thought she should do well."

I was shocked to hear such nonsense. It was bad enough if the doctor were lying to give Murida false hope, but if he believed what he said, it was much worse. Who had taught him this? I later learned that "it was his personal experience." For Murida, I managed to hold back my disappointment and annoyance.

When I was young, I'd heard a lot of superstition around healing. I'd contracted polio when I was just a year old, and Mother had been desperate to find a way to make me better. When I was twelve, a natural "healer," or so-called "traditional Arabic doctor," had visited the family home, promising to help me walk again. My father, a realist, kicked the man out.

Perhaps in part because of this experience, I was always disappointed to hear pseudo-scientific ideas on health, especially when they came from doctors.

The next morning, I heard that cancer victims should not eat red meat, only fish and chicken, because red animal meat was like human tissue and so it nourished the cancer cells. Once again, I held back my annoyance and anger.

That same morning, I went down to the pathology department. The tissue was finally ready for interpretation, and I introduced myself to a kind young pathologist, explaining that I was a skin pathologist visiting from the U.S. The two of us examined the slides together.

I was unhappy to see that the cancer was present throughout the whole breast, not only in small nodules as the oncologist had told Murida. The more I looked, the worse I felt. This diffuse infiltration was a bad sign. It explained the retraction of Murida's nipple, which she'd noticed several months prior to the lump. It was as if a force had begun pulling her nipple inwards long before Murida became aware of the lump.

Worse yet, the cancer had spread to eleven of the sixteen lymph nodes removed from Murida's left axilla.

She must've had cancer for a long time, I thought. Only frequent mammograms would have changed my sister's fate. It was common practice in the United States, of course, but not in the UAE. Health-care delivery was very different in the Emirates: People generally visited the doctor only when they felt ill, and preventive tests were done only among the highly educated and financially well-to-do. Mainstream education skipped over most health topics. With the prevailing conservatism, education about a "breast" disease or "cervical" cancer would not make it to radio or TV. In this, the Emirates were quite different from Lebanon, where sexual issues were discussed on live TV. If Murida had continued to live in Lebanon, I thought…. But such thoughts were pointless.

Once I was done looking at the slides, I thanked the young pathologist and left, stumbling down the hallway, my mind stuck on the image of cancer "everywhere." I didn't go back to Murida's room, because I couldn't face her, not yet. First, I had to clear my head and quiet my heart. I had to overcome my own disappointment before I could give false reassurances to my sister.

So I went to the garden and sat on a bench in the searing July heat. I didn't mind the heat. On that day, there was a little breeze and almost no humidity. In truth, it felt good out there, as the hospital was kept excessively cold. Besides, it warmed my cold, insecure soul. I looked beyond the hospital grounds, out to the desert, and was surprised not to feel anything. Usually, I was mindful of the natural landscape and squeezed out all the joy I could from the beauty of nature. But now I was barely moved by my physical surroundings. I could think only of Murida's fate and my role in it.

As I sat on that bench, I couldn't deny that I was in some way responsible for my sister's situation. I was the family's only doctor, and I should've told my sisters about preventive tests, including mammograms. As I'd looked through the pathology slides, I couldn't lie to myself. If I'd told Murida to get annual mammograms, she would've done it. But I'd never engaged any of my siblings in discussions about preventive medicine. They sometimes called for advice, and I gave it. But I never thought I was responsible for everyone's health. Was I? Was it possible that each of my seven siblings, as well as our parents, expected that I would make recommendations for them, tailored to their individual ages and gender, for the rest of their lives?

They probably did, I thought, even though no one had told me so. Even if no one spoke the words aloud, this didn't relieve me of the responsibility; after all, I was the only doctor in the family. As I'd looked through the slides, I felt mixed up. My mind said *you are not responsible,* but my heart said *you are.*

I felt wretched. I could've saved Murida's life if I'd just asked her to do a yearly mammogram. But perhaps she wouldn't have wanted to spend money on one each year, since she was spending so much on other tests? Or she might've been reassured if one test was negative and stopped after that. Was I responsible for reminding her and every other sister as well? I continued to debate the issue in my mind for the rest of the day, and would do so for years to come. I never reached a conclusion.

After a while, Murida's youngest daughter, Ghina, began to feel anxious about why I hadn't returned. She searched through the hospital and finally found me sitting on the bench.

Ghina stood in front of me, a little breathless. "Why didn't you come back to the room?"

"Sit by me," I said. "I need a moment outside the hospital. I get melancholy if I don't get enough light each day. I even use a special lamp on my desk."

Ghina sat down and also looked out at the desert. She was one of my favorite nieces—I loved her nontraditional and feisty nature.

"How do you think your mother feels about her cancer?" I asked.

"She's optimistic," Ghina said. "We all are. The surgeon, who's Palestinian, said he took the whole breast and all the lymph nodes out, and the total body x-rays showed that all the internal organs and bone were normal."

Before I could say something, Ghina continued.

"And, just to be on the safe side, she'll get chemo and radiation, too. There is nothing else that can be done, right?"

"True. But she seemed so sad and concerned."

"She's been through a lot. And you know Mother—she's cautious and she can't take things for granted. Because of her life, you know. Nothing's come easily for her."

"I know," I said. "She's a hero."

For a moment, the two of us sat in silence.

"So what was the result of the pathology?" Ghina asked.

"To tell you the truth, I was surprised. The cancer is present in the whole breast and eleven of her lymph nodes."

"Is that very bad?"

"Maybe"

"But they took it all out—the surgeon said so. I saw it myself, there's nothing left. She has a line of sutures from the middle of her chest to her armpit. Thirty-three."

"I know." I touched my niece's hand. "Hopefully she'll be okay, especially since she's getting chemo and radiation. And hormone treatments as well."

"Hormones"

"Her cancer is the type that would be susceptible to hormones. They'd already finished that test by the time I got down to pathology. And that's good, because hormone therapy is just pills. They're easy to take, without serious side effects."

"So why do you look gloomy?" Ghina asked.

"I just didn't expect it to be in so *many* of her lymph nodes. I wish they were clear."

"What does it mean?"

"Well, once the cancer has reached the lymph nodes, some cells may have already escaped into the blood stream." I didn't tell my young niece that some of Murida's organs might already be seeded with cancer. Even if I'd been asked directly, I probably wouldn't have admitted it.

"What will you tell Mother?" Ghina's face tightened. "You know she's waiting for you."

"I'll be positive. I'll emphasize that it's all out and that the future treatment will destroy leftover cells if there are any."

"Good," Ghina said.

Like her two oldest siblings, Ghina had been clever in school. But Ghina was also unique among Murida's children: She was forceful in asking for what she believed to be rightly hers. Murida sometimes thought that, if she had been born thirty years later, she would be like Ghina. For that reason, and many others known only to the two of them, Ghina had a special place in her mother's heart. Ghina loved her mother's company and was proud to be seen with her mother just as she was proud of her mother's accomplishments. She could not manage to be as proud of her father.

Yes, Saleem was Ghina's father, but it was her mother who'd made sure that the children ate well and succeeded at school. *She* raised them. He was so often an obstacle, yelling and threatening to hurt himself. Unlike her siblings, Ghina knew that he was bluffing, which was why she never cried or ran after him.

Ghina sometimes wished that her mother would stand up to her father. She knew many women who weren't her mother's equal, and those women were treated better by their husbands. Ghina knew her father had been deprived as a child, but that was no reason to make her mother pay.

As well as being the most self-assured of Murida's daughters, Ghina was also the least religious. I thought that, if Ghina had grown up in a less religious country, she might have been agnostic, like me. Neither she nor Manal ever wore a headscarf. Mona reminded her littlest sister to pursue her faith, but Ghina seemed to have lost the thin thread that connected her heart to faith.

Finally, I picked up my crutch and walked with Ghina back toward Murida's room. I leaned my right hand on Ghina's left shoulder for a little extra physical support. As we walked, I realized that there was nothing wrong with being more hopeful than reality dictated. My sister should feel hopeful so that she could enjoy herself and not live in constant worry. If she was destined to get worse, then she would deal with it as it happened. Living in anticipation of bad things served no good purpose.

If I'd been the one with cancer, I would want to know exactly what was going on. But honestly, what was the point of that? Hope was better. Yes, I decided,

I needed to imbue my sister with hope. Just as "mercy is better than judgment," so hope was better than reality.

I remembered studies that showed how people of faith fared better after a heart attack than those without, especially if they received the moral support of a priest. That sealed it: I must let Murida live in hope for whatever remained of her life.

Outside the room, I put myself in the right mood for speaking to the assembled family. I entered the room and put on a happy smile, as if my sister was recovering from something simple, like gallbladder surgery. I suddenly remembered the good mood in the room after our father had gone through hernia surgery at the American University in Beirut hospital. I'd watched the surgery, which had gone well. Afterwards, under the influence of anesthesia and pain medicine, our father was visibly happy and even making jokes, and saying for the first time that he loved his children, especially Muhiba.

"It's all out," I told Murida. "You definitely needed this surgery so you could get rid of the small cancerous tissues."

"What about the lymph nodes?" Amal asked from her seat on the wall facing her mother.

"Some were affected, but not all." I turned to Murida and decided to tell a white lie. "You know that lymph nodes are what limit the spread of an infection or a cancer, stopping it from reaching the blood stream and other organs. The lymph nodes are a sort of a gatekeeper or a filter. Like a colander."

Amal looked up, her brow furrowed. "So is it good that they have cancer?"

Ghina leaned forward, her hands pressed together. "What *khalo* is saying is that her lymph nodes worked well to stop the spread of the cancer."

After that, there was only one way I could answer: "Exactly."

Murida worked hard to smile. "Thank you, *khayya habibi*. God keep you for me, and for all of us, and may He keep your boys and wife safe from all ills."

"*Ya rab*," Amal and Saleem said together.

"Do you need anything?" Saleem asked me.

"Tea, if you can."

"Of course I can," Saleem said. "I know all the nurses, and I give them all candy. Do you want some?"

Saleem dug a handful of hard candy out of the pocket of his white galabeya and offered it to me, and I took one. Saleem urged me to take more—after all, he said, he could get more.

"Murida," I said. "You seem to be doing so well that you might be able to go home tomorrow."

"But she has a drain," Amal said. "And they're measuring the volume of fluid she takes in and what comes out from the drain under her arm."

Mona stepped into the room from her seat by the hallway. "We can do that at home. I just talked to the nurse and she said that the 'fluid balance' has to continue for several days, until there's no drainage any longer. It might take a week, but it doesn't mean mother has to stay in the hospital for the whole week."

"I agree," I said, "and you don't want to stay in a hospital longer than needed, since you can catch an infection here." I turned to my nieces. "It's better for Murida's spirits to be in Sharjah with one of you. And I know the four-hour drive every day is disruptive for you and for Mahmoud."

"Okay," Murida said. "Let's just stay until tomorrow."

When she'd asked to stay another day, Murida had something particular in mind. Since the day before her surgery, she'd been taken to another wing of the hospital for an hour each day. That's where she saw a psychiatrist.

In Twam, it was routine practice to provide patients with psychological support after traumatic treatments, and this was especially true of women who had undergone mastectomies. Murida's psychiatrist was an Egyptian man in his early forties, dark-skinned, short, with a smile that allowed Murida to relax as soon as she laid eyes on him. He talked, and she listened. He addressed her as "Mama," since she could have been his mother.

Murida wished he were her second son or perhaps her brother—he was so kind, gentle, and respectful.

He asked how she felt. She didn't hide that she was sad and wondered aloud, "Why me?" He said that her feelings were all normal and expected, that he saw this all the time with cancer patients, while reassuring her that she would slowly recover and get back to a normal life. She nodded and said *inshaallah,* God willing. She believed him and looked forward to their visits.

This was not the first time Murida had troubles with sadness or even the first time she'd seen a psychiatrist. It had started right after Murida delivered Amal, and it hit her like a storm. So, every now and again, Murida took a small dose of Xanax, just half a pill to rest her sad and irritable soul. She knew many others who took it, and they hadn't lived through even a small fraction of Murida's troubles.

My sister Suad talks about her nerves and medications in public, and she hasn't experienced half of what I have. I wish I had her courage. But we have different personalities. I keep to myself, and she lets it out.

Even our toughest brother, Mutasim, had suffered a nervous breakdown while he was working in the Emirates, away from his family during the 1982 Israeli invasion of Lebanon. Everyone knew about it, even though no one talked about it in public or even asked Mutasim how he was doing. Murida also remembered how, as a child, I would cry on winter evenings for no reason.

If she'd asked, I would've been happy to tell her that, even as an adult, I had to deal with anger and anxiety. Even our youngest brother was affected during the war, when he was terrified to sleep at Mutasim's empty apartment, which he did so that militants wouldn't occupy it. It didn't seem likely that Mahmoud could stop a forced entry by armed men, but, being the youngest Mahmoud had to obey a lot of orders from Mutasim, as we all did.

Still, Murida thought, no one needed to know. They might think less of her and her children. Muhiba in particular couldn't know—she would hold it against not just Murida, but also against Ghina. If Muhiba would mock Murida's hearing loss, Murida imagined it would be even worse if her older sister knew that Murida was seeing a psychiatrist. I wished I could tell her that Muhiba also struggled, and was no happier than she was.

CHAPTER FIFTEEN

The next day, Murida visited Dr. Ramzi. After that, she ate her lunch before the nurses came to change her dressing one last time as Mona and I watched. I felt sad that my sister had gone through such major surgery—her left side was now deformed. Instead of removing just the lymph nodes, the surgeon had removed her whole axilla with the overlying skin. The nurses gave Murida a bag of medications with instructions on how to take them, a bag of dressing supplies, and a container to measure fluid intake and output. The nurses wished Murida well and thanked her for being a "good patient." Murida and Mona thanked them profusely.

Murida, Ghina, and I left the hospital in Mona's car. In a second car, Mahmoud drove his father back to Sharjah. For the next few days, I would stay at Mona's along with Murida and Saleem. I would sleep in Tala's room, while Murida and Saleem would stay in the boys' room. It was a difficult time, and the next few days were overwhelming.

By the time Murida got back to Sharjah, it seemed as though every distant relative, new friend, and old neighbor had been informed of her surgery, and they had all begun to arrive at Mona's house to do their duty by paying a visit to the sick. Some also came to see me.

In addition to all these new visitors, Murida's children came every day, along with their spouses and sometimes their children. My sisters Suad and Ilham also came every day. In an attempt to lift Murida's spirits, and to avoid the topic of cancer, most people acted as if they were there for a social visit. Some talked about politics and the stock market. Others talked about TV shows, movies, religion, and other people. They avoided talking about cancer and, most of the time, they didn't even address Murida directly. They didn't know what to say to her and were worried about accidentally saying something that might hurt her feelings.

Murida sat in a large, soft armchair, looking out through the wide glass windows, feeling sick of the large gathering. *I am a private person,* she thought. *I hate that anyone besides my own children might be imagining me without a breast. It's not their business.*

As was customary, each of the guests stayed for hours, so that the house was never empty. Mona had to attend to them all day: making tea, coffee, and sometimes snacks for the children. *This is not a coffee house,* Murida thought, *it's a home. Leave me alone. You are tiring my lovely Mona.*

Despite Murida's wishes, the guests continued to come for days. In the morning, Murida would haul herself out of bed, get dressed, and come out to Mona's living room.

Our sisters came every day. *They want to see Diya more than they care for me,* Murida thought as she watched our sisters talk. Suad and Ilham were never close to Murida, and they had never showed her the kind of respect girls show an older sister. *They showed it to Muhiba because they're scared of her. Everyone is.* Muhiba was tough, so she got her siblings' respect, whereas Murida was always the less assertive, less fortunate sister.

It had been a long time since Murida had been really connected to our sisters. She'd decided years before that she had to focus on taking care of herself, her children, and Saleem. She had just enough energy for that. She wasn't angry with our sisters—she'd just lived for her own family. Murida was startled out of her thoughts when my gaze met hers, and I smiled at her.

She must have felt a flash of guilt, as I could see it move across her face.

As for me, I enjoyed the company and praise of so many people that I rarely saw, some who'd grown up near us in the camp. I didn't think much about Murida's prognosis. I postponed that until the last moment.

After six days with my sister, I was set to fly back to the U.S. The evening that I left, the family held a small gathering at Mona's home. My flight was at 2 a.m. and Mona's family, Murida, and I stayed in the TV room until midnight. At the end, I stood up and hugged everyone individually. I kept Murida until the end, because I wanted to have a longer goodbye with her. But as I was moving to hug her, she quickly kissed me on both cheeks. But I still went on and hugged her—actually, I squeezed her. Neither of us cried. I had not yet let my feelings sink in, and was still playing the doctor's role.

"Do you think I'll live long enough to see you again?" Murida asked.

I was surprised that she was so pessimistic. I suppressed a trace of fear and pessimism and said "of course," insisting that I would see her the following year.

"God willing. Do you really think I am going to be okay, *Khayya?*"

"Of course," I said again, reflexively wondering if my answer was false.

Mona and Saleem reiterated my wish, *inshaallah*.

On my way out, I felt a sudden emptiness in my soul that left me feeling the same anxiety and gloom I'd felt as a child during the short days of winter. The trip had brought me close to so many people who I loved and who loved me, as well as new ones I'd learned to love. Now I would be away from all this. Fortunately, I had two sons and a wife to soothe my aching heart. I suddenly realized that I had not said goodbye to Tala.

"Where's Tala?" I asked, turning to Mona.

"She's hiding in our bedroom, crying," Mona said.

"Why?"

"She doesn't want you to leave."

Over the previous days, Tala and I had grown particularly close. I always liked intelligent and determined children, particularly girls, particularly when they were my nieces and their daughters. Life was unfair to Arab girls, and I considered them my soulmates in suffering.

Tala was only thirteen then, but she kept me company. She'd made me tea and coffee and eaten cheese and zaatar pies with me at the kitchen table. I encouraged her to become a doctor—she had the intelligence and the right personality. We agreed that she would specialize in pediatrics. She liked that I was funny and not afraid to show it, that I wasn't "serious" like so many older men. I'd made them laugh in spite of Teyta's illness. I even sang for her.

I called toward the door. "Tala, don't you want to say goodbye to me?"

Tala, still weeping, called back from the end of the long hallway. "No, I don't want you to go."

"It's okay," Mona said, shaking her head. "She's not coming out."

So I left without saying good-bye. It wasn't the warmest visit I'd ever had to my sister, but it might've been the most packed with emotion.

The best time that I'd ever had with Murida was during the week I spent with her family in December of 1982.

By then, Murida and her family had been in Dubai for five years. After six months of living in the midst of the death and destruction of the Israeli invasion of Beirut, I was happy to be in a peaceful atmosphere, among my sister's family. Around twenty people met me at the airport and competed to drive me and have me stay with them, but I'd decided before my arrival that what I wanted most of all was to spend time with my dear sister Murida. By then, I was strong enough to easily climb the stairs to the second floor. After all, in Beirut, I had to climb stairs to the sixth floor when there was no electricity to operate the elevator.

Every day, we went out and had a picnic. We played on swings, sat by the water, and grilled meat in the park. Murida and her children showed me the original Dubai landmarks that had nearly disappeared twenty years later, after the Emirate had been built up like New York and Singapore.

Maha was already at university, so she spent most of her time studying. Mona was sixteen then, and she played music and danced for me, and we became friends. The two of us talked about music, and Mona had a little-known recording of one of my favorite singers. On my last day, Mona gave me the precious tape, and I took it with me to the U.S. and listened to it for the next twenty years until it came out on CD.

In every picture taken during that week, Murida was smiling. She showered me with love and respect and made all my favorite meals. I admired her tenacity in the face of so many of life's difficulties. How amazing it was that she'd raised seven well-behaved, smart kids! Murida was my mother without the drama, my big sister, and my friend. I'd even enjoyed Saleem's company, as Saleem also loved music and knew many songs and carried a tune well. He wasn't as stupid as people thought, I decided.

In this loving environment, I even regained a little of my lost faith. I understood how people who grew up surrounded by religious teachings could become so faithful.

Before I left the Emirates in 2006, I'd been given one last responsibility: telling our mother, Fawziyya, what was going on with Murida. Since our father's death eight years before, Mother had been living on her own in Beirut, assisted by a live-in maid from Sri Lanka.

I girded myself, as I knew that our mother would likely have a "hysterical" reaction. Fawziyya knew that I'd traveled to the Emirates in order to be with Murida after a surgical procedure, but she didn't know the extent of her daughter's illness. She didn't think it could be cancer. Even if she'd been told it *might* be cancer, she would've refused to believe it. Her strongest daughter could not get a fatal illness. Not yet.

I imagined and re-imagined Mother's reactions as I prepared to call her. All her stories about life and death, which I'd heard many times, were etched in my mind: how she'd lost an infant daughter in 1946; how she'd lost a son during a difficult delivery thirteen years later; how she'd lost her father to a simple eye surgery.

It took a great deal of effort to pick up the phone.

I knew, as I picked up the phone, that it would be impossible for Mother to accept that Murida could die first. That wasn't supposed to happen: Parents should die first, that was life's rule. Fawziyya remembered what horrible pain her eldest daughter, Muhiba, had gone through when her son Waleed had died twenty years earlier. And Fawziyya had lost two babies already. Even at eighty-five, she still counted them as "my children."

Mother's third girl had been named Kifaya, or "enough," at the request of her mother-in-law, who had insisted on the name, saying it would be a sign to God that three girls were *enough,* and it was time for a boy. After all, why should young Fawziyya continue to produce girls? Badr's other daughter-in-law had boys in abundance.

Fawziyya hated hearing her mother-in-law praise this "mother of the boys," as if a woman could determine the sex of her babies. Fawziyya had loved her daughter Kifaya, who resembled her. But one hot summer day, when Kifaya was six months old, she had diarrhea, perhaps because of some adult food given to her by her grandmother. This was when the family still lived in Palestine, and Fawziyya still helped out in the fields with the tobacco crop.

In the morning, Fawziyya had placed her sick infant daughter in the care of her mother-in-law. When Fawziyya returned in the evening, Kifaya was dead. Had Badr not kept an eye on her? Had she not given the baby enough sugar water so that her body had dried up in all that heat?

Kifaya's death remained a mystery. It tortured Fawziyya for several years before she forced herself to stop thinking about it. What was the use of questioning? She hadn't caused her daughter's death. If she'd thought that Kifaya could be in danger, she would've asked permission to stay by her daughter's side. Ultimately, Fawziyya let go of the guilt. Or perhaps it turned into a new feeling—that of hatred for her mother-in-law.

The second death, this time of a baby boy, left Fawziyya with a different kind of scar. She was thirty-eight and ready to deliver. For the first time, at the midwife's advice, she went to a hospital. But in spite of strong labor, Fawziyya wasn't making any progress. Because the baby was large and also breech, the hospital staff felt they couldn't save both the mother and baby. The doctor went to my father in the waiting area and asked him to choose between his wife and his child.

So, while exhausted from labor, my mother watched the staff kill her son by squeezing his head through her abdomen and tearing up her tissue. When she saw his beautiful face, she was devastated. She was shocked when my father explained that to deliver him alive she would've had to be cut open and possibly die. It was a normal surgery elsewhere, but the UN-contracted hospital that served Palestinian refugees was not equipped for such a thing.

Those two incidents, and my polio, were plenty of pain for our mother.

"Hello, *habibi*," Mother said, when she picked up the phone. "How was your trip to Dubai and how is Murida?"

I could hear that my mother was concerned, but she preferred not to hear bad news. I assured her that Murida was fine.

"What does she have? They said that she had something removed from her breast. Why?"

"She had a lump in her breast, and so she had it removed and tested."

"So was it the good kind, God willing?"

No, I told her.

"What do you mean? *It's not the good kind?*"

"She'll need more treatments to make sure it doesn't come back."

"You mean 'that disease'?"

"Something similar," I said, in order to avoid uttering the word cancer.

"Oh my God, why her? Hasn't she had enough in her life? Where did she get it from? Why?" My mother started to cry.

I let my mother say all she needed to at such difficult news. Then I told her that Murida would receive chemo and radiation, and that afterwards she would be cured. I knew I was lying, a little, but I felt it was for a good reason. If I'd told her the plain truth, she might've gotten hysterical. Besides, with a little miracle, perhaps Murida would live. And our mother was eighty-five. A shock could be bad for her.

"Chemo is terrible. I remember when Waleed got chemo—he got sick and died after only three months."

"Waleed's case was much worse."

"Some people do well. The Khayri woman is still alive after twenty years."

"Pray for Murida."

"You know I do, with every prayer. I ask God to protect all my children one by one."

"And please remember when you talk to her not to cry so that she doesn't feel worse. It's very important not to make her feel that she's in danger.

"Oh my God, my Murida"

After the conversation, I hung up, feeling momentarily relieved.

CHAPTER SIXTEEN

After my trip to see Murida, I talked often with Mona and Mahmoud to get news about Murida. I also called Murida every week or two to reassure her and to answer her medical questions.

So it was that I heard about her first, uneventful chemotherapy session—Mona called me from the car on their way back. The nurse had found a good vein in Murida's right arm, and the infusion had lasted less than two hours. On their way out, Murida expressed surprise at how easy it was.

"Thank God," Murida told Mona, "I don't feel bad at all."

"Thank God for his mercy," Mona said. "He's keeping an eye out for you. I told you that He won't leave you to suffer alone. In a blink of an eye, the next six treatments will pass."

After the treatment, they drove back home, and Murida was almost happy. She had passed the biggest first step in a seven-step journey. She even felt like eating for the first time in two months. She wanted a big pan of fried eggs, fresh warm bread from the bakery across the street, olives, zaatar, and labneh. She wanted breakfast food for an early dinner. She would make it all herself in Mona's kitchen—Mona wouldn't mind. Mona would feel good that her mother was eating at last. After that, perhaps she would take a nap.

In the last few months, Murida had gotten used to naps, something she'd never done in the past. But now her sick body seemed to need it and, for the first time, she was obeying her body.

Two hours after Murida's meal, as the sun was setting and the mosque was declaring the time for evening prayer, she woke up feeling terribly nauseous. She ran to the bathroom and threw up. Mona heard her mother and came over.

"Do you think one of the eggs was spoiled?" Murida asked.

"No. Remember what the nurse said about nausea from chemo? It can take several hours to appear."

"Oh my God, it feels like knives are cutting into my stomach."

"Lie down," Mona said, "and I'll get you a Seven-up. They say it's good for nausea as long as you drink it in small sips. And I'll call the pharmacist downstairs."

"Please get me something."

The pharmacy delivered anti-nausea medicine, but when Murida threw up again ten minutes later and saw the pill in the vomit, she got discouraged. On the phone, the pharmacist said to take another one. After taking a second pill, Murida rested, drowsy from the medication. She woke up only once during the night feeling nauseous, but there was nothing in her stomach to throw up. In the morning, she woke again, exhausted.

"How do you feel now?" Mona asked.

"Weak, but thank God less nauseous. That was worse than the pain of surgery. The nurse said that I might feel nauseous, but I never imagined how bad it could get."

"Last night I spoke with Samia, whose mother had chemo for colon cancer. She said her mother used to take a nausea pill with each dose of chemo, and she took one every six hours after that. I'll ask them about that for the next round. They must have assumed we would get it on our own.

In four or five days, Murida felt well enough to take a two-hour taxi ride to Abu Dhabi with Saleem. There, she would spend time with her oldest daughter and confidante, Maha. Murida spent two whole weeks at Maha's. She got several calls a day from each of her other children, and, on weekends, many of them made the two-hour trip to see her.

Ghina was there on the first weekend. For Murida's youngest, it didn't matter where her mother was—she had to see her every week. Every Friday, like the call to prayer, Ghina collected her kids and went to her mother's, homework and final exams notwithstanding.

When Ghina saw her mother, she smiled. "They say chemo causes baldness, but look: Your hair is perfect."

"Don't jinx it," Maha said.

"I'm just saying that maybe everyone is different."

"I hope so," Murida said.

"It's two o'clock," Rafiq said soon after Ghina had arrived. "Shall I go get dinner?" He turned to Murida. "What do you feel like?"

"You don't have to trouble yourself, I'll eat anything. What do you have, Maha?"

"We have nothing. You know Maha isn't the cook that you are," Rafiq said. "I'll go buy dinner from the Lebanese restaurant. Why don't I get roast chicken, kafta, and hummus?"

"That sounds great," Maha said.

Rafiq returned with two bags of wonderful-smelling food, and they all got excited, especially Maha's three daughters. Everyone loved the food from this particular restaurant which was as good as the best restaurants in Beirut. They had dinner—the adults and Osama at the dining table and the children in the kitchen. Ghina had made a cake for dessert and brought it all the way from Sharjah. They had tea and coffee back in the living room while chatting and watching TV, until the time for evening prayer when Maha and Rafiq each went to a room to pray. Murida and Saleem followed.

Although the children were separated from the adults at this meal, for the two weeks that Murida stayed with her eldest daughter, whenever her grandson Osama was home from the dorms, he did not let his grandmother out of his sight. He was even more protective of her than his sisters.

Osama was Maha's eldest, Murida's first grandchild, and he loved my sister in proportion to how much she loved him. Murida had been the primary caretaker in Osama's first year of life, when Maha was still attending al-Ain University, two hours away from home. While Maha stayed in the dormitories, Murida lovingly cared for Osama, until Maha finished her education and moved to Abu Dhabi. That day, Murida felt a hole had formed in her heart. She missed the little boy so much! He had revived her mothering instinct after a rapid succession of births left her little room to enjoy being a mother.

After Maha took Osama and moved to Abu Dhabi, Murida would always send Osama his favorite foods with anyone traveling to Abu Dhabi. She was a second mother to him, a mother who didn't ask him to study or behave. She loved him just for being him. He could've written a book about his grandmother: how much she meant to him, how often he thought of her, how he asked God to heal her with every prayer, just as he was sure she asked God to help him succeed and remain healthy.

Murida called Osama daily at home and later at college, and treated him like another son. She didn't count a day as finished unless she had spoken with Osama: It was a comforting part of her routine. She risked annoying Saleem, but talking to Osama every day was one of her great pleasures. He helped by being a grateful grandson. As a child, Osama hadn't realized that he and Murida had a special relationship. But as he grew to have many cousins, he realized that Murida treated him as "the chosen one." He studied hard in order to please her. He went into engineering in order to impress her. Osama loved and respected his parents, just as Murida and the Prophet would want him to, and he was gentle with his sisters, just as Murida would have wanted. But now Murida was more than just a grandmother, she was a near-saint. Osama decided that God must love Murida, which was why He'd chosen to test her with cancer. If she passed, she was sure to go to heaven.

The day before Murida returned to Dubai, in order to ready herself for the second chemo session, she took a bath at Maha's house. Murida had only been in the bath for a few minutes when Maha heard a loud gasp. By the time Maha got to the bathroom door, the gasp had changed to weeping. Maha knocked on the door and entered to find her mother looking at a thick bunch of hair clutched in her right hand.

"Mother!"

"Look," Murida said, continuing to weep. "I lost my hair in one wash, like plucking feathers from a chicken in hot water"

Maha didn't know what to say.

"How could this happen? Look, I'm bald."

Murida pulled out the rest of her hair just by rubbing it, one clump at a time, her tears mixing with the hair, the shampoo, and the water on her face. Maha stood just inside the doorway, shocked, not knowing what to do or say.

Tears sprang into Maha's eyes, and she tried to hide them in order to appear strong, as Mona and Mahmoud said she should. But Maha admitted she was weaker, more sensitive when it came to her mother's suffering. Suddenly, Maha began weeping, first quietly then loudly, synchronous with her mother. She didn't feel guilty for crying. How could anyone expect her to hold back her feelings at a time like this? She wasn't made of stone!

After few minutes of crying, Maha and Murida stopped almost together. Maha couldn't look into her mother's eyes. Murida was balder than her own very bald father, and she looked alien with the skin of her head exposed. She was silent, staring at the floor of the tub, where all her hair was clumped. The hair looked not at all sorry for leaving Murida's head.

After a short while, Murida came out of the bathroom looking despondent, her headscarf suddenly too big for a head that had just a few loyal hairs remaining. Maha got a pill from her mother's bottle of Xanax and offered it to her. Maha felt like taking one herself. Murida welcomed Maha's offer and swallowed the pill. An hour later, she was rested and relaxed. She was still sad, but less overwhelmed, and she was glad she'd taken the pill. She sat in her armchair, drifting in and out of a sleepy state. Maha offered to help her get into bed, but Murida liked this state of mind and didn't want to interrupt it. Besides, if she took a real nap, she might not be able to fall asleep later.

During the next two hours, Murida had many visions. For most of those two hours, she was peaceful, except for a recurring image of herself walking in the street. She walked, and a gust of wind came to blow off her scarf and expose her bald head. Fortunately, in the vision, there was no one else in the street.

Murida couldn't explain the vision, but by the time she woke completely, she'd come to accept her baldness. She thought i*f this is the worst that chemo does, I will accept it willingly.* She knew that her hair would grow back. Mona and Ghina had both said so.

All she wished was that the staff had warned her about a few things, especially about how much her left arm would swell. No one had said that it would nearly double in size, and it felt so heavy that she had to lift it up with the right. It didn't even look human any longer—it looked like the arm of a giant sea creature she'd once seen on TV, or the fattest woman she'd ever known, a woman who sold sweets in the refugee camp.

The arm was nearly useless, and Murida dropped even small things. One day, she'd dropped a large knife on the kitchen floor, and it had fallen very close to her foot. The nurses had said she should do physical therapy at home, but despite exercises and massage, the arm continued to get bigger.

Murida wasn't like her older sister Muhiba, who had the light brown hair and light skin so desired in our community. Murida had curly dark hair and olive skin and was seen by most to be the less beautiful sister.

Then, after she had her children, Murida's appearance changed: She gained weight and became the only overweight Mutasim girl. But she was so self-conscious about her weight, both because of her appearance and its effect on her health, that she regained her normal weight in less than a year. As she aged, her appearance almost didn't change: She was slim, yet her face had no wrinkles whatsoever. She was flattered whenever someone said how pretty or how young she looked. "Are you sisters?" some asked when she and Maha were out together. She would share that with her daughters and smile.

During the next session, the doctor gave Murida an anti-emetic while she received her chemo. She became smart about taking the anti-nausea pills, swallowing one at the first sign of distress. But by the next day, she felt tired, had no appetite, and had a metallic taste in her mouth. Her face was also red and warm. She later learned that the change in her face was because of the steroids she was given along with the chemo. It made her remember an asthmatic neighbor in the camp, whose face was also red from all the steroids the doctor gave her, and our sister Suad, who swelled up when she had to take cortisone pills and shots as a young teenager.

During the third course, Murida experienced what chemo doctors often feared: She had no healthy veins left in which to receive the chemo infusion. They had to call in "the expert," a young Palestinian man who was their best at inserting IVs. He was extremely kind to Murida and was finally able to locate a small vein. Murida thanked him profusely and asked him to please be the one who got the needle into her arm every time. Except for once, when he was off, he complied with her wish.

The IV expert once told Murida that she reminded him of his mother in the West Bank, not just by her appearance, but by her kindness as well. He'd been trying to get his mother to move to Al-Ain and live with him, away from the Occupation, maybe even find him a bride. Murida, who was impressed with his serenity and kindness, pleaded with God to deliver his wish. If she'd had a single daughter, she would definitely have married the girl to that man.

The fourth through the seventh courses of chemo brought progressively worsening difficulties and side effects. My sister's veins, which grew small and clogged because of previous treatments, became her biggest fear, and she thought and talked about them the day before and all the way to the hospital. When I heard about it from Mona, I wondered why they hadn't placed a permanent chemo access into a large, deep vein, as they did in the U.S. After all, that surgery would be minor compared to what she'd been through. But, after some reflection, I chose not to tell my niece about it. If the hospital did these procedures routinely, they would've done it for Murida. If not—it was better that the family didn't know. This was a policy that I often adopted in dealing with patients who couldn't receive the best available care for financial or other reasons.

Following each of the final four chemotherapy sessions, Murida developed painful mouth sores and could barely eat. When she could, food no longer had any taste. She called me to ask for anything that might help, but she was already using what I recommended, with little benefit.

After the last session, Murida couldn't hold back her feelings any longer. She wept as she said goodbye to Rami, the nice IV man, and others at the hospital who she'd come to know during the five months of chemotherapy. These were people she now thanked for having been part of her healing. Yes, they'd caused her pain, and she'd suffered from weakness and nausea, but in the end she saw them with new eyes. Now, she saw them as enablers of her healing. She was surprised by the sense that she would miss them. When she returned for radiation treatments, she would have to stop by and say hello.

Despite the side-effects from chemo, during the five months of treatments, Murida's life had regained some semblance of normalcy. She would have a treatment, and then there were three weeks for her to recover. She'd spend the first week with one of her daughters, and then go back to her own house for the next two weeks. Each daughter insisted that Murida spend at least a week with them. They each wanted to spoil her, and she let them. It wouldn't be fair to refuse. Helping one's parents was required by the Quran and the prophet Mohammed, and it weighed heavily in God's decision on whether or not a person went to heaven. Each day, they gave her fresh juices, fresh vegetables, and fresh fish. On good days, Murida was able to laugh, especially at Ghina's jokes and silliness. Like me and her aunt Suad, Ghina did not mind laughing at herself.

Whenever Murida was able to laugh, she felt good twice: once from the laughter and once as she realized that she was now able to laugh. Ghina cheered her, because Ghina had the emotional energy of the young and the wisdom of an introspective mother. She was a progressive in a conservative community and a youthful spirit among women who felt and acted "old" once they became mothers.

By the time Ghina finished high school, al-Ain University was no longer available to non-Emiratis. So Ghina and her three sisters had to get their college education by studying at home and taking exams at the end of the year at the Beirut Arab University built and sponsored by Egpytian President Gamal Abdel-Nasser. But Ghina stopped soon after she got engaged, as she realized she would not work once she had a baby. Ghina was angry that she hadn't gotten a chance to obtain a proper education, so she escaped into books, mostly international literature in translation. She learned from reading, but became yet angrier when she compared her life to that of the books' heroines. She could've been any of them, experiencing a life much richer than her own.

Even though Ghina read widely, all this didn't impress her poetry-writing father-in-law, who still wouldn't show her love or respect. Murida had long thought that Ghina's father-in-law would show Ghina respect, and perhaps even love, if Muhiba allowed it. He was a gentle man who had a large capacity to love—but he loved his wife first and would do only what she wanted. For a long time, Murida had wished her sister's heart would soften. Life was too short to keep a grudge.

Two weeks after Murida finished chemo, Mona and her husband joined Mahmoud and his wife on a trip to Mecca to carry out one of their five duties as observant Muslims, the haj. Murida asked the four of them to pray for her at the Kaa'ba. She didn't have to ask, as that was one of the main reasons for the trip: Murida's children wanted to get closer to God in order to ask Him to forgive and bless them, and to heal their mother. Murida thought about her children throughout the two weeks and prayed that God would accept their prayers. She felt serene when they called and told her that they'd all prayed for her more than once.

After they returned, Murida started radiation treatments at the same hospital. Again, the first treatment was uneventful, although that wasn't true of the rest. She spent most of January and February dealing with pain at the radiation site: the left side of her chest and her underarm. The skin turned black and sloughed off. She applied the salves that were provided, but they didn't make it any better. The pain was sharp and continuous, like a bad burn. She took pain pills, but those didn't help, either.

"My skin is charred," she told me the phone. No one had warned her about that. It made me wonder if she was getting the wrong dose of radiation, as it seemed to be more than a simple case of acute radiation dermatitis. But she decided she would tolerate the pain if it would eliminate the chances of cancer coming back.

Still, she wanted little comforts. She asked me when she would have a night's sleep without pain.

By mid-March, 2007, Murida was fully recovered from the ill-effects of radiation. The only thing that reminded her of the cancer was her swollen left arm and her absent left breast. Even her hair had grown back. Now, she dared to plan for the future.

CHAPTER SEVENTEEN

I
t was a Friday afternoon, and the Dubai spring was growing warm, ushering in the famous summer heat of the Gulf countries. It had been a full year since Murida noticed the lump. Murida welcomed five of her children—the ones who lived in Sharjah—into her home. They came along with their spouses, but didn't bring children. Murida had made several dishes, and she wanted to celebrate with her family. No, she wouldn't call it a celebration. It was just an opportunity to repay her children and their spouses for the care they'd given her when she needed it. She was especially grateful to her sons-in-law, who weren't obliged

to keep her in their homes. The only one who had a responsibility to take her in was her son Mahmoud.

Murida cooked her sons- and daughter-in-laws' favorite dishes: stuffed baby zucchini, stuffed grape leaves, roast chicken with eggplant and rice, raw kibbe, tabbouli, and hummus. The men and two of the women sat around the formal dining table while the rest took places in the adjacent living room. They chatted and managed to laugh. It was almost like the old days, when Murida would regularly invite everyone over for a big feast. They finished the meal with tea, coffee, fruits, and the sweets that Murida's daughters had brought.

For the first time since her daughters had left home, Murida allowed them to clear the table and wash the dishes. She didn't even feel bad about it. After all, she'd been able to let go of some of her pride in the previous seven months. Her daughters had already cared for her many times. That genie was out of the bottle— there was no reason to put it back. Besides, they would be rewarded for all this loving care in heaven.

In Murida's struggle between holding on to her pride and accepting help, the latter had won. *She's changed*, Mahmoud thought, *and sometimes change doesn't mean giving up on your principles, but adapting to the inevitable.*

As Murida looked at her children at the party, she felt saddened that she'd had to go through cancer treatments before she could accept help from others, even from her own children. She'd expected them to help with housework from the time they were young. But the moment they got married, she liberated them of their household "duties" and refused any further help. They belonged to their new families after that, not to her, and whatever time or help she got from them was a bonus. She wouldn't require anything more—only Mahmoud still had an obligation to her and to Saleem. In this she was different from our mother, who asked her married daughters to do housework every time they visited.

For the first time since the illness had fogged up her brain, Murida felt aware of her feelings. Now she could look within herself and recognize where she'd been and who she'd become. The past year had been long and full of dramatic events, both physical and emotional. She was proud of herself for having been through so much without losing faith. She didn't look back on what she'd gone through, only on what lay ahead.

The weekend after the big dinner, Murida, Saleem, and some of the children and their families traveled to a resort on the beach just an hour's drive away. The children wanted to celebrate the end of their mother's treatment. They all wanted to celebrate her new life.

The little ones had a wonderful time swimming in the pool and in the waters of the Persian Gulf, and Murida loved walking on the beach with Mona and Ghina. In Beirut, we'd lived just a mile away from the sea, yet she'd never gone to the beach, since "good" Muslim girls didn't do that when she was young. Now, she loved the open skies over the water, far away from tall buildings of Dubai. There was a lovely breeze, and few people were around. They were almost alone at the beach: There were just a few "shameless" Russian tourists sunning in their skimpy swimsuits on the other side of the resort. Murida was shocked to see a woman lying on the sand, face-down, without a top.

Food at the resort wasn't bad, Murida thought, considering that it wasn't homemade. And there was an abundance of fresh tropical fruit juice made to order. Murida felt strange that no one had to cook or clean. Was this how rich people lived? She wouldn't be happy living like this forever, yet she wished the trip would never end. She felt closer to God being next to his creations—the wide seas, blue skies, and fine powdery sand. They should come back, Murida thought, maybe even twice a year. She would be willing to spend her own money and spare her children the expense. It would be worth it.

Everyone except Saleem was happy with the vacation. On the third day, Saleem insisted on going back, as he missed his home and friends. "What can a grownup do in this sort of place, anyway? There's no one to talk to."

"That's how it is supposed to be," Ghina said. "It's a resort."

Saleem grew loud and shouted at Ghina for attempting to talk him out of returning home. "What do *you* know?" he said.

Mona's husband intervened. "Abu Mahmoud—"

Before Mona's husband could finish his sentence, Saleem interrupted. "It's not your business."

"Yes, it is," Mona's husband said. "You came along knowing that we would stay for five days."

"And now I want to go home."

"All right," Mona's husband said. "Go home. Take a taxi."

"Murida should come with me. She's my wife."

"You said you miss your home and your friends, not Murida. What do you need her for?"

"For whatever," Saleem said.

"You're staying in a nice resort—you eat when you want and sleep when you want. No one's asked you to do anything but enjoy yourself."

"What?"

"Are you so selfish that you'd ask your wife, who's just finished seven months of painful treatments, to go back with you? I really don't believe my own ears."

"Then don't."

"How could you ask her to go home with you instead of resting here, without having to worry about housework?"

Saleem was silent.

Mona's husband shook his head. "No. She won't leave."

This conversation took place in full view of all the adults, as the children swam in the pool by the beach. Murida felt furious. She was furious with her husband's selfishness and lack of social tact, furious with Mona's husband for treating his father-in-law with so little respect, and then furious with herself for pitying Saleem. She realized that Mona's husband was saying only what was on everyone else's mind. Still, she thought, Saleem should not be scolded in public.

That was bad. But even worse was the time, a few years earlier, when Saleem had behaved so cruelly with Murida that Mona had asked her mother to leave him.

Saleem's tongue-lashing had been fierce, and Murida had run away into her room and closed the door. She'd tolerated and supported this man for years and now he was insulting her. This was too much. After a short while, Mona called, and Murida could not hide it from her.

"You shouldn't accept this," Mona said. "Leave him. Let him feel how he'd be without you. You've taken more than enough."

"Where would I go?"

"You can live with me or Mahmoud. Or you could stay some time with each of us."

"He's still the man of the house. What would I be without him? I know he's hard to deal with, but that's how he's always been, ever since I married him."

"But it could ruin your nerves."

"I have thick skin, and I can deal with him. At least I have a man. It would make some people pleased to see me divorced—you know who. I couldn't let that happen."

Mona knew who her mother meant. Whether or not my oldest sister would really be pleased to see Murida divorced, Murida would never want to look smaller in her sister's eyes. And it would be a shameful disaster for our parents.

"Anyway," Murida added, "I can't leave him, because he would be a burden on you and your sisters and Mahmoud. Don't ever mention this again."

When I heard the story from Mona, I felt overwhelmed by how much Palestinian women had to endure. It was Palestinian men who talked so much about the loss of *their* land, and *their* pride, but it was women who had to endure the biggest emotional consequences of these losses. Where did they get the strength? Murida suffered through all that Saleem had, and then also allowed him to feel that he was the family's true leader.

At the beach, Saleem had finally agreed to stay "one more day," but in the end he stayed the remaining two. He must have felt embarrassed, Murida thought. Or perhaps he'd called Mahmoud and complained, and Mahmoud had told him to stay for Murida's sake.

All that spring, Murida allowed herself to experience happiness. She enjoyed her time with her children and at her home. She even slept peacefully. Once her head hit the pillow and she said a few prayers, she went into a deep and uninterrupted sleep. She finally could taste the flavors of the foods she ate. She was more mindful of experiences that she had previously taken for granted or performed out of habit. She learned how to savor the moment.

Could the doctor be right? She wondered. *Could I live at least five years like this?* It was perhaps too much to expect, although God was capable of anything.

How sad it is that a person takes so many joys of life for granted until she feels that her days are limited. Maybe some of heaven can be experienced here on earth. Murida was happy to have come to this realization.

All of us in the family remember the spring of 2007 as the time Murida was almost back to her old self—except maybe she didn't laugh as much as before. Murida would not forget the wise men's lines that "after each hill is a valley," "after happiness will come sadness," and "life gives you one happy day and takes another." She tried not to flaunt the goodness, hoping that the badness to come wouldn't be too bad.

CHAPTER EIGHTEEN

Towards the end of June, Murida caught a cold that seemed to be going around. But while everyone else recovered in less than a week, Murida did not, even though she took the same remedies as everyone else. "Maybe it's because of your immune system. I read that chemo weakens the immune system," Ghina said one Friday afternoon as she saw her mother struggle with a persistent cough. "Maybe you have bronchitis. Remember when I had the same thing two years ago?"

The cough was accompanied by rapid breathing and shortness of breath, symptoms that Ghina had not experienced. Saleem could hear each of his wife's noisy breaths during the night, and she was breathing faster than usual, with one breath falling directly into the next.

If Murida didn't sleep with her head elevated, she would feel as though she were drowning. She also felt weaker than before, and had to sit down once or twice while cooking a meal. Her first thought was that she was developing asthma. She had seen one of her granddaughters struggle with her breathing, and the doctors said it was asthma. *Where did I get asthma from?* she wondered. *I never had it before.*

It wasn't easy to hide her symptoms from her children. Even while talking on the phone, she had to take a breath in the middle of a sentence. Mona thought that her mother might have caught pneumonia, as her immune system might have been compromised by all the strong drugs. She told Ghina maybe their mother needed antibiotics. Maha and Mahmoud also expressed concern.

Finally, Murida's children decided that she needed to see a chest specialist and perhaps have a chest x-ray. When they were visiting one Friday, they all managed to recommend it after Murida had a long and painful bout of coughing and gasping that frightened Maha.

Ghina and Mona were the ones who arranged for Murida to see a lung specialist. It was an Arab woman, and Ghina had heard good things about her. Upon listening to Murida's chest, the doctor suspected bronchitis. Pneumonia was less likely, she said, since Murida didn't have a fever. Next door to the doctor's office, Murida got a lung x-ray and a bottle of cough medicine. The doctor promised to call the following day with results. The cough syrup helped Murida sleep— it must have a sedative, she thought. Muslim scholars warned against traces of alcohol in cough syrup, but Murida didn't let herself think about it.

Murida didn't let her weak lungs slow her down. After the chemotherapy and radiation treatments had finished, my sister discovered that there were so many things she wanted to do! During the trip back from the beach, she told Mona and Ghina that she wanted to go to Beirut to see her mother, who'd been so anxious and concerned about Murida's condition. She wanted to check on old neighbors who hadn't been lucky and still lived in the crowded camp. She also wanted to visit our aunts and uncles, and our sister Muhiba.

Murida also wanted to tour the places she'd never been before. Gulf citizens flocked to Lebanon in the summer—why couldn't Murida do the same? After all, she'd grown up there, but had barely left the neighborhood around the refugee camp. Like our parents, she took her family on a one-day picnic along a river in the mountains every summer. That was the landmark event that they talked about for weeks afterwards.

Thanks to Mahmoud, Murida even had an apartment in Beirut that was just a few minutes' walk from

Mother and across the road from one of our aunts. She planned to visit our mother every day. Yes, she'd cook for her and listen to her. After all, our mother was a talker, and Murida was a patient listener.

Although there was tension between our mother and Muhiba, there was none at all between Mother and Murida. Mother's second daughter obeyed parental wishes as if she were still living at home.

Mona and Ghina both said that they would go along on the trip, and surely Manal and Amal would as well. Murida planned to visit our dear father's grave. In the past months, she had missed him more than ever before. She set a date—the first week of July. By then, it would be too hot to do much in Dubai, and her grandkids would be finished with school. The whole family could travel!

Murida spent the late spring of 2007 in the bliss of planning for the future. She started packing the gift items that she'd received over the years to furnish the Beirut apartment—dishes, fancy glasses, towels, tablecloths. Her daughters had given her some lovely things, and she was keeping it all for Beirut. She wanted a lovely place there, not less than Muhiba's.

During the blissful early spring, Murida also visited her daughters more than ever before, and yet she never felt like a burden. Now, she was just like everyone else: cancer-free. She'd gotten the triple treatment—surgery, chemo, and radiation—and there was nothing else to be done. She was even taking daily hormone pills to halt the growth of any remaining cancer cells.

The only other thing Murida wanted was for someone to tell her "you're cured." If only someone would say it—but no one did, and she didn't dare ask. As long as she didn't ask, she could believe what she wanted. Hadn't the fancy x-ray tests failed to show cancer anywhere else? Hadn't the surgeon told Mahmoud and Mona that she would live at least five years? Murida had the right to believe that she was in the clear.

Unhappily, those days didn't last. It wasn't long before Mona picked up the phone and heard the new lung doctor's voice on the other end.

They exchanged pleasantries, and the doctor hesitated for a moment. "I think you should take your mother back to Twam."

"Is it…cancer?"

"A simple x-ray can't confirm cancer, but what the specialist saw on the x-ray couldn't be anything else. She has a lot of fluid surrounding her lungs, so much that they couldn't see the lung tissue itself clearly. But fluid means cancer in her lungs is very possible. She'd need a CAT scan to confirm. I'm so sorry."

Mona choked, barely managing to get out a brief thank you before she hung up. She wished the doctor hadn't said she was *sorry*. Without that word, Mona would've had a little hope that it wasn't cancer. After a short moment of confusion, sadness, and lost hope, Mona hurriedly dialed her brother.

As soon as Mahmoud answered the phone, Mona tried to suppress her crying and speak normally. "It is…in… her lungs."

After a stunned pause, Mahmoud began to weep. Mona didn't hold back after that, and it was several minutes that they sat on the phone, listening to each other cry. After they hung up, Mona did the same with Ghina, who yelled out in anger and frustration before she fell into despair, "Why? Why?" Ghina was angry at the whole world, at God, and at all people who didn't have cancer, including her own relatives.

By the time she called Maha, Mona had run out of tears. "Why, God?" Maha asked. "What did she do? She did everything they asked, and she's just started to feel alive again. She put her life on hold for so long. Ya Rab, help her."

Maha thought that her mother hadn't lived a single day between the time of her diagnosis and when the treatments had finished at the end of February. For seven or eight months, Murida had just been surviving, doing her duty to her body. Life had been deferred, put on hold with one purpose in mind: getting clear of cancer. Every time there was a reason to be happy, Murida had thought, *I'll enjoy it when I feel fine.* Murida's age, Maha thought, was sixty-four years minus those lost eight months.

Everyone in Murida's family was shocked by the cancer's spread to her lungs. After she'd finished her five months of chemo and six weeks of radiation, Murida had been told that she was guaranteed to live five more years. At least, that's what she and her children had understood from the doctor.

When I heard about this, I wondered if the doctor had been talking about the "five-year survival rate" of patients like her. But Mona and Mahmoud insisted that the doctor had said "your mother will live for at least five years." Suad, who had been nearby, confirmed what they said.

So why had Murida's body not responded in the way it was supposed to? She ate so well—the best foods for cancer patients—and she prayed for health every day. Was it her bad luck again? I struggled to provide a satisfying answer. In the end, I had to tell them that it was just a random event, bad luck.

CHAPTER NINETEEN

Maha suggested that they shouldn't tell their mother what the doctor had said. But Murida would need to be treated—they couldn't delay that. So someone had to tell her, but not right away. Everyone was shaken. They decided that Mahmoud would tell her something the next day. He wouldn't tell her that she had cancer in her lungs, only that they needed to do another check—a CAT scan, which was a complex and expensive test—so she had to go back to Twam, where all her records were.

Murida's children were more angry than sad. They'd gotten used to being sad, but the new collective emotion was that of anger, frustration, and despair.

Hadn't they paid their dues by being refugees in Lebanon and working guests in the Emirates? Wasn't what they'd already been through enough?

At Twam, Murida's symptoms and the x-ray report immediately raised the doctors' suspicions. Knowing Murida's case, they were certain it must be cancer in her lungs. So they aspirated fluid from around the lung. Aspirating the fluid would relieve the pressure on the lung, and the fluid could be sent for testing.

This time, Mahmoud and Maha went with their mother to the hospital. Mahmoud drove from Dubai, and Maha took a cab from Abu Dhabi. Soon after getting Murida into an available bed, the staff had her sit on the side of the bed as they cleaned her back with antiseptics. Mahmoud stayed and held his mother's hands, but Maha couldn't watch the procedure—she couldn't tolerate her mother crying out in pain, nor could she bear seeing a large needle inserted into her mother's back. She was almost certain that she would faint, so she left before they started. She hadn't realized the procedure would be so painful that she'd be able to hear Murida's cry from the end of the hallway. She found herself crying. Maha had never heard her mother cry in agony like this, screaming for mercy.

Murida cried out as, with every millimeter of insertion, she felt something tearing into her body. They said it would be numb, but she felt the needle go all the way in. They finally placed a tube into the hole they'd made and taped the tube to her back. The tube was connected to a bag that would collect her lung fluid, which was slightly turbid with hints of pink. As the fluid filled the plastic container, Murida felt suddenly better and could breathe more easily.

"I had all this in me?" Murida asked.

That evening, when I called, Murida asked how she'd gotten that much fluid in her lungs, and I had to explain that the cancer was in her lung tissue. The cancer cells must have reached the outermost part of the lung, which was wrapped in a thin double membrane. That's why she had fluid: The membrane cells reacted to the invading cancer cells by becoming inflamed and secreting fluid.

After the fluid was drained, the doctor told Murida that if the cells in the fluid were cancerous, then she would require chemo. Murida's heart sank at the word "chemo," and she became dizzy. She felt suddenly despondent. After her return to Twam, she'd suspected that cancer might be involved, but those suspicions hadn't felt real until that moment.

What Murida didn't know was that the decision to re-start chemo had already been made based on the x-ray and the physical examination. There could be no other explanation except that cancer had spread to her lungs.

It took a long week of waiting for the fluid test to prove that cancer had spread to Murida's lungs. By the time she was informed, she'd already received her first dose of chemo. She was also connected to oxygen through a tube that came out of the wall and was placed in her nostrils. My sister hated that tube. It was a nuisance, both physically and aesthetically. It dried her nose and caused painful scabbing. Plus, it made her look sick when she didn't feel that bad. *Oxygen is for the very ill,* she thought. *It's for those in their last days, which is not true of me.*

But oxygen made Murida breathe more easily and feel better. During the week that the fluid was being tested, Murida held on to the possibility that it might not be cancer. No one knew how she held onto such false hopes. She didn't know, either. But hope and faith were such strong weapons against fear that she had no choice but to use them.

During that week, Murida received many calls and visits. Our mother called and cried on the phone. Murida hated it when she saw or heard anyone cry, but hearing Mother cry was the worst. Not only was Murida causing her eighty-five-year-old mother pain, but crying meant a loss of hope. She knew our mother didn't control her emotions well and must feel awful, but she wished Mother would stop crying, for Murida's sake. *It's a bad omen,* Murida thought.

But her most difficult conversations were with our oldest sister Muhiba.

Muhiba was the only person whose calls consistently made Murida cry. It was the same every time: Muhiba was kind, and she always said, "He who gave it to you can take it out of you." But the moment Murida heard her sister's voice she choked up and remained silent. As her sister spoke, Murida struggled to stay quiet, but she could never hold her emotions in for long. Soon, Murida would start crying, and she would keep crying after Muhiba hung up.

Murida never understood why Muhiba had such an effect on her. The two had never shown much affection towards each other, and they hadn't felt much love for one another, either. On the contrary, members of the Mutasim family had long been aware that the two eldest Mutasim sisters were jealous of one another, or perhaps just did not care for each other. Muhiba never let Murida think that they were equal—after all, Muhiba thought she was prettier and she'd married the better man. Her children had lighter skin and more access to their grandparents, since they lived nearby rather than in the poorer, more remote part of the camp.

Murida's children didn't understand why their mother cried so much when Muhiba called. They wondered if their mother was crying because she felt inferior to Muhiba, since she was now so sick. Perhaps Murida was even hoping and waiting for Muhiba's visit.

Or was she just touched by Muhiba's affection after so many years without it?

In the end, they agreed it must be the latter. They were surprised and saddened: They were surprised that their stoic mother, who'd never admitted that she needed anyone's support, finally admitted to needing the affection of her older sister. And they were saddened that it took sixty-four years for their mother to receive the affection that she seemed to have wanted so very much. Murida didn't know that she was not alone in her need and that many of our siblings were too proud to admit they yearned for affection. Our parents hadn't left us time or space to express our feelings, as we were supposed to focus solely on studying and work as they struggled to keep us in clothing, food, and schools.

In September, after Murida was finished with another, shorter course of chemotherapy and felt almost normal, she invited all her children to dinner. Maha traveled from Abu Dhabi to be with them. Murida had a special lamb meal in the freezer, and she insisted on cooking it against their advice—they didn't want her struggling to prepare a big meal. Did she think that, if she waited any longer, she might not have another chance?

Murida's children didn't think that was the reason for the meal until Maha told them that Murida had asked whether, if she died, they would all visit her grave and read from the Quran.

"She also asked if I thought Father would visit her gravesite every week and say that he missed her," Mona said.

Mona realized their mother must be thinking of the end. So, a few days after the meal, Mona invited Murida to do a philanthropic act. Mona wanted her to choose such an act while she was still alive. Murida and Mona went to an Islamic Philanthropy office, and Murida gave money to dig a well in poor Afghanistan. Murida also wanted to build a mosque in another poor Muslim country. She asked Mona to take her savings and ask me to add what was necessary to finish the project.

If Mona hadn't suggested it, Murida probably wouldn't have thought to give her small fortune to charity. Murida didn't know anyone from the camp who had done something like that—even among people with more money to spare. Our father had become religious during the last year of his life and had given more than his share to the needy and poor in the camp. But he didn't pay for digging a well or building a mosque. No one would have expected Murida to do what she did.

It was also September when doctors found that Murida had brain metastasis. The doctors ordered a scan and confirmed it. Yet, to her children's surprise, Murida was not upset. She even told Maha that she didn't mind it as long as she had no symptoms. No one talked about it—they didn't even tell me, the family doctor—yet no one understood Murida's indifference to such a dramatic turn of events. Was Murida living day by day? When I learned of it two months later, I thought maybe she'd changed more than I'd thought she could. If it were me, I would have lost hope or lived in fear of sudden death. Thankfully, Murida must not have been told the possible consequences of having a growing mass in one's brain.

Indeed, Murida was concerned about her breathing more than anything else. She hadn't told her children that she was feeling short of breath again. By early October, Murida was no longer living at home, as she needed help all the time. She spent few days with each child. And I had to make another difficult call to our mother.

"Mother," I said, after some small talk, "you should go see Murida."

"Why now?" she asked. "I thought she was better. She was planning to come for a visit."

"She's okay, but I don't think the doctors will let her travel. So you need to go."

"Is she going to die? Like Waleed? Tell me the truth."

"You know Death's timing is in God's hands and no one knows," I said. "But I'm going, and I'll see you there."

"Okay. I'll talk to Muhiba. I'll need a visa."

"I'm sure you can get a visa."

"God willing"

That night, our mother couldn't sleep. She loved my hard-working, uncomplaining sister, the daughter who never yelled at her or took her father's side.

It was true that Mother had hoped for a boy while she was pregnant with her second child. But she'd accepted Murida—the quiet one, seemingly satisfied with the little attention she got.

After her third daughter died in infancy, Mother became attached to her second daughter, little Murida. Could she lose another child? No, she thought: Murida was strong. As the years went by, and our mother's stomach illness appeared to be chronic, she looked to Murida as her healthy echo, the one who would balance her own feebleness. She could count on Murida.

Unlike Muhiba, Murida did not complain. She did just what her mother hoped and wanted. If she ever resented it, no one knew.

CHAPTER TWENTY

It wasn't long before our mother flew out to Dubai, a few days before the end of October. She got off the plane on a wheelchair and was taken straight to my older brother's home, as tradition required. That's where she settled in, and that's where she was when she called Murida, who was staying at Manal's.

The call made Murida anxious. She knew that our mother wouldn't leave home except for a grave reason, and she realized I must've told Mother that Murida was very sick. Our mother was eighty-six, and she'd not left home since our father had died nine years before. Everyone knew about her fear of the elements, especially the sun and the wind.

It's not right that an eighty-six-year-old should visit a six-ty-four-year-old, Murida thought, *or that a mother should visit her dying daughter or even that someone leave Beirut to visit Dubai. It's supposed to be the other way around.*

Murida was also anxious because Mother was so emotional—she held back neither her feelings nor her words. Murida wasn't looking forward to our mother's visit, and the thought made her feel guilty. This was her *mother*, after all, and she'd already made the trip. Over the phone, Fawziyya said that she'd come to Manal's house later in the day. Murida reprimanded herself and hoped for the best.

An hour or so after the first phone call, Mutasim called Manal from the street. He wanted Manal to come get her grandmother from the building entrance, because he had to go to work. Ghina, who was at Manal's that day, went down and brought her grandmother up. Murida heard the door open and felt her heart racing, her breaths coming faster, her mind suddenly alert.

Upon laying eyes on her mother bent over from osteoporosis, Murida had an entirely new feeling. She felt sorry for our mother. Murida would be an emotional burden—she, the strong one, who had done so much for the family! It would be a complete role reversal, except that Murida's mother couldn't be the caretaker. She might even add to the burdens that Murida's children were already carrying.

Ghina held her grandmother's arm as the two walked slowly into the family room. Since Fawziyya had fallen and broken her wrist twenty years before, she walked carefully, and with such a curved back that her head was no more than four feet from the floor. Once Murida and her mother locked eyes, Murida felt a mixture of fear, sadness, and also relief: fear of her mother's reaction, sadness for her mother making the long journey, relief that the difficult moment had arrived and would soon pass. At last, they'd met. As our mother walked towards Murida could tell that mother's face was full of anguish and grief. Her lips twitched.

Murida's mother reached out for her daughter's hand, lifted it up, and kissed it.

What is Mother doing? Murida wondered. *People kiss the hands of "blessed people" or of their parents, not their children. Is Mother already considering me a saint? I haven't died yet.*

Just then, our mother began to cry, "God, why my daughter Murida? She doesn't deserve this."

No one else said anything. After another short moment, Mother leaned in. "How do you feel? What do the doctors say?"

Before her grandmother could say anything else, Ghina interrupted. "Can I put your food in the kitchen?" She knew that Murida would have a hard time responding to Fawziyya's questions, so she interrupted the flow of questions and changed the subject. She also knew that her grandmother was planning to stay for a while, which meant that she'd brought her special food. Everyone knew about grandmother's diet. She ate four meals a day, always at the same time, always the same foods, with a few minor variations.

"No, it's okay. I'll eat soon."

Amal and Mona arrived shortly after. They could tell their mother was stressed, so they took over the conversation and questioned their grandmother about Beirut, about neighbors and relatives, and about Muhiba. Fawziyya was happy to oblige them. After dinner, Murida took a nap. Our mother fell asleep while sitting up, which happened often, since Fawziyya didn't think going to bed for a nap was a good idea.

Three days later, our sister Inaam flew in from Amman. Despite her tears when she'd first heard about Murida's condition, Inaam didn't weep or look shocked at Murida's decline. Indeed, everyone present—including Murida—was surprised at Inaam's apparent lack of emotion. I thought unhappy Inaam must've learned to hold in her feelings.

Although Inaam and Murida were only four years apart, they had never been particularly close. By the time Inaam entered school, Murida was in her last year, and soon she became the family's housekeeper. But Inaam had loved Murida, who was so much gentler than their oldest, critical sister and appreciated the small things in life.

When she turned twenty in 1968, Inaam left Lebanon for her second adoptive country, Jordan. Inaam had been just six months old when my family first fled their town in Palestine. I was fifteen when Inaam got married, and I clung to the car that took my sister from our camp home. For the first few years, she visited every summer, until the Lebanese civil war prevented her from coming.

When Inaam visited, Murida was busy raising five or more children, so their relationship didn't have a chance to grow. Their lives intersected again when Murida and Muhiba's first-born sons, Mahmoud and Khaled, both wanted to marry Inaam's oldest daughter. In the end, Inaam decided not to give her daughter to either cousin. She had grown critical of girls marrying their cousins and considered her own unhappy marriage as proof.

The day after Inaam arrived she went with my mother to see her sister, who was then staying at Mahmoud's. When they arrived, Murida was taking a bath. Suddenly, they heard Murida shout for Mahmoud. After finishing her bath, Murida discovered that she wasn't able to lift herself up out of the tub. Her left arm was useless, and her right arm and legs were not enough. Mahmoud helped lift her up, and Ghina dried her and helped her get dressed as Murida grieved the loss of her strength.

When she came back to the living room, Murida addressed our mother as if she was giving a public speech: "See me. I can't lift myself up. See what happened to your strongest daughter?"

Mother tried to calm her down. Inaam was shocked, but did not show any emotion.

But whether or not she still had any strength left in her body, Murida still intended to do her social duty. If she was still alive, she would repay her family's visits.

So, two days later, Murida asked to be driven to our brother Mutasim's house. She wanted to perform her duty of greeting Mutasim's son, who had just arrived from Canada after completing his engineering PhD. Murida also needed to repay her mother's and sister's visits, she said, as they too were staying at Mutasim's house. Mona was surprised and tried to talk her mother out of it, but to no avail.

Murida got out of the car at Mutasim's building and was immediately short of breath. A few minutes after arriving, her cough and breathlessness worsened, and everyone asked her to go home to rest. They were all surprised that she'd left home in the first place, and Mother even reprimanded her.

"But it's my duty," Murida said, wishing her brother continued success for his sons.

After Murida left, Inaam had tears in her eyes. She could not fathom our sister's respect for tradition. *How sweet*, Inaam thought. Most people had stopped following such old traditions.

Murida grew up in a time when abiding by tradition was very important. After losing their homes and country, Palestinians held onto their traditions very tightly, and this was particularly true of those who'd come from small agricultural towns like Tarshiha. For those of us who lived close together in refugee camps, it was still possible to honor these traditions.

We Palestinians visited each other on the birth of a child, on the holy days, for illness and death, for the arrival of a traveler or a husband who worked in another country, and for graduation or the passing of the national exams in high school—especially when it was a first-born son. We attended weddings, as well as pre-wedding celebrations: dance, music and henna painting by the neighborhood girlfriends of the bride-to-be.

Murida grew up in the early days of the Palestinian diaspora and learned to respect tradition. Her mother emphasized doing the right thing, which meant following tradition. Even when others didn't do their social duties to her, she kept doing hers to them. As the newer generations of Palestinians shed their traditions one by one, Murida stuck with hers as long as she could.

Two days later after her disastrous visit to Mutasim, Murida was at her daughter Amal's house. Mutasim had come with his son to repay Murida's visit, and Ilham was there, too. As Murida sat in her chair, listening to them talk, she began to feel as though she were drowning. Her lungs seemed to be full of fluid, and her face turned purplish. She began gasping for air. It was fortunate that she didn't look at the eyes of those around her. If she had, she would've seen several people preparing to say goodbye. The others were scared, shocked, and at a loss. Everyone thought it was the end. No one knew how to respond. Mutasim later told me that he'd never been so close to death as he'd been that evening, even when he had visited his nephew Waleed in his last days.

But suddenly, like a choking victim who's successfully received the Heimlich maneuver, Murida coughed out some stringy substance and suddenly felt better. Although I wasn't there, I thought it might've been a portion of a tumor in the lung that had broken off and temporarily obstructed a major airway. The family decided that she should go back to Twam in the morning, and made hurried preparations to return. Everybody present had their own explanation of what was next for Murida, but no one said a word. The words "death" and "the end" would have had to be uttered, but no one was willing to do it yet.

As they left the next morning, Amal's kind husband Fahmi stressed that he wanted Murida to return to his home as soon as she was out of the hospital.

"We'll be waiting for you," he said as they drove off. He loved the company of anyone related to his wife, especially his kind and quiet mother-in-law.

As for myself, I'd planned to visit the Emirates during the Thanksgiving week. That way, I could be away from work for only three days yet be away from the country for a week. But, once I heard the news about Murida choking, I realized that I no longer had the luxury of time. I hurried to change my reservation and left Wednesday, November 14. I'd spoken with an oncologist friend of mine who told me that Murida's days might be numbered, and I hoped that my sister wouldn't die before I arrived.

On my way, I called Mona from London, asking if Murida was still alive. Mona was shocked by the question. A few years later, she would confess that she'd thought that my call from London had been overdramatic. At that point, Murida was fully conscious and talking. She'd even gone to the bathroom by herself. Mona hadn't thought that her mother's situation was so serious. Ghina hadn't passed on what her husband Khaled had said: that Murida's present case reminded him very much of his brother Waleed's final days.

CHAPTER TWENTY ONE

I arrived late on a Thursday and, the next morning, Amal drove me to Twam hospital. We stopped at Starbucks so that I could get a quick cup of coffee, which was three times more expensive than it was in the U.S. Amal played an Um Kulthoum classic song and was still able to do small kindnesses: She gave me the CD to take.

I tried to imagine what Murida would look like. I imagined her just as she'd been a year and a half earlier, but now with a tube of oxygen in her nose. Once we were outside Murida's room, my pulse was hurried and I could scarcely breathe.

As I opened the door to Murida's room at Twam, I recognized it immediately. It was a mirror image of the previous room. Her bed was on the right this time and, as I'd expected, she was connected to oxygen. Besides appearing swollen and slightly pale, everything else about Murida was the same. Unlike other cancer patients I'd seen, Murida had not lost any weight. Her daughters sat on chairs lined up along the walls of the room, looking gloomy. No one had a trace of optimism on their faces. Some seemed on the verge of crying.

Murida was fully awake and aware, and I thought that was a good sign. It was only on the way to the hospital that I'd been informed that she'd had brain metastasis since the summer. This was also when I learned that the children had told her that the doctor would give her a stronger medication as soon as I arrived. My shoulders sank as I approached her bed.

I knew my sister was tired of the enormous effort it took to breathe. She could barely finish a sentence without having to stop to take a breath. And when she had to go to the bathroom without oxygen, she felt that she was choking. But as much as she needed the oxygen, she also hated it.

I stood by my sister's side and kept repeating those false, reassuring words that had come to my tongue so often in the previous year, when discussing her cancer, and then sat by my sister on the edge of the bed.

As I held my sister's hand, I felt that I was holding ice. Her skin was pale, clammy, and freezing cold. I went to the nurses' station and asked the nurse to take Murida's temperature and vital signs. I also went through her medical record, which the staff let me access once they knew I was a doctor from America. I was shocked to learn that Murida's liver was extensively involved with cancer. Her liver enzymes were ten times the normal levels. She was also receiving morphine to ease her breathing and to sedate her, as she had become quite irritable and anxious all the time.

None of Murida's children had been told that the cancer had spread to the liver. They were shocked and became despondent—the cancer had taken over. It had won, and Murida had lost. Ghina, who'd kept me company since I arrived at the hospital, seemed to suddenly lose hope.

I also felt helpless: If the cancer was in these three important organs—the brain, lungs, and liver—then it must be the end. There was no turning back. This idea was further cemented in my mind when the nurse told me that Murida's temperature was just 31 degrees Celsius or 88 degrees Fahrenheit.

I knew that this wasn't the cold of death, but instead the cold of a severe systemic infection. I'd learned long ago that the most likely source of sepsis was the urinary system, especially in women. It turned out that Murida had a urinary tract infection that had spread to her blood stream. She was immediately started on strong intravenous antibiotics. I explained to Murida's bewildered children that the temperature regulating center in Murida's brain must not be functional and, instead of getting a fever, she had developed hypothermia.

I felt certain that it was the end, but how could I tell my sister? I couldn't—and wouldn't. But I decided I *would* be honest with her children. I told Mahmoud, Mona, and Ghina, but they didn't accept it. They were either in denial or truly didn't believe me.

Then I had an idea. My sister was already receiving morphine—ten milligrams every three hours—but she was getting only slightly sedated. Maybe a larger dose would relieve her of her anxiety and irritability. Yes, it would be risky, but that was a good way to die if it happened: quietly and without suffering.

So after sorting out the antibiotics, I asked to meet the oncologist. He was a gentle, mild-mannered Arab man in his early forties.

"You probably know," I said to him, "that Murida has sepsis and is severely hypothermic. So with lung, brain, and liver metastases, she must not have long to live."

"Only God knows."

I was disappointed that the doctor had already brought God into the discussion, and gritted my teeth.

"So can we make her last days comfortable? I mean by increasing her sedation."

"If you mean to accelerate her death, effectively killing her with a morphine overdose, no we don't do that here. It is against our Muslim principles. Only God decides when it's time for a person to die. I know in America you do that, but we don't do that here."

I thanked the doctor and walked off, realizing that there was no chance of finding common ground. Mahmoud had overheard the conversation and told his sisters. Mona was the one who approached me.

"Uncle," Mona said, "we don't agree with what you're thinking."

"But your mother is suffering."

"The Quran says that God tests those he loves, and the more someone suffers on earth, the greater their reward in heaven."

I said that I understood, although in truth, I neither understood nor accepted this opinion.

While Mona was certain in her belief that good people went to heaven, I hadn't been sure about that for a very long time. Indeed, I didn't believe in heaven and hell, or a life beyond what people experienced on Earth. I believed in something close to Indian karma, but thought it played out on earth—not in the afterlife.

Even when I'd had faith as a child and a teenager, I never gave much thought to the afterlife. I believed that death was the end of the deceased, who would leave behind only his effect on others, good and bad. Many times, I had wished that I could regain my childhood faith, but it hadn't happened. Even when Father died, my attempt to reconnect with my faith had failed.

The next day was Friday, and many visitors were going to the prayer rooms in Twam hospital or the nearby mosque. I stayed in Murida's room, where I watched the expressions on each visitor's face as they came and went. I was always interested in how people reacted to difficult situations. It was the same part of me that loved movies and books, and the same part that made me consider psychiatry as a specialty before I fell in love with dermatology.

As I watched, I saw that one of Murida's daughters seemed frightened. She didn't seem as scared of losing her mother as much as of death itself, I thought. Another daughter looked sad in anticipation of losing her mother, and her face had the expression of someone who was saying goodbye. A third daughter acted with a stern and steady attitude and touched her mother often. I thought she must be strong internally or acting strong for her mother's sake. I wished everyone could behave that way, including my own sisters.

I knew how perceptive Murida was and how easily she could read what was on her children's minds, including their fears. I wanted Murida to have hope until her last breath. I knew it was a false hope, but its effect on her spirit would be the same. People lived for years with false hopes, so why shouldn't Murida have false hope for a few more days?

After lunch that day, Murida wanted to go to the bathroom. Following the doctor's orders, the nurse offered her a bedpan. The nurse had been told that Murida should not leave bed—she would be too unsteady both from her condition and from the morphine. But Murida refused the nurse's offer of a bedpan with such intensity that, for the first time, the nurse accepted a patient's decision over the doctor's orders. The nurse offered to help my sister to the toilet, but Murida firmly refused this as well, with a sweep of her right arm. Only her children could go with her to the bathroom, she said. So, with her arm connected to a hanging bag full of antibiotics, Murida was helped out of bed by two daughters.

Maybe I should've been proud of her determination, but I felt saddened that my sister was still holding onto her pride at such a late hour. I wished she would let go: of her pride and of her life. I wished that she would stop fighting, but how could she stop? She'd fought all her life for everything she had. I thought that, if the positions were reversed, I would likely do the same, although I hoped I could learn from my sister's experience: that there was a time to live and a time to die. I hoped that I might act like our father, who welcomed death six weeks after my long-awaited first child arrived.

On Friday evening, I learned that there was a new doctor on call and would be for the next two days. This new doctor was Scandinavian, and he listened to my thoughts with respect. He admitted that Murida was dying and that it could be a matter of hours or days. He also promised that he would increase the dose of morphine in order to make her feel more comfortable and allow her to breathe more easily and fight less. He also noted that she would need more oxygen because her lungs were severely and diffusely invaded by the cancer. None of Murida's children were close enough to hear this conversation.

Late Saturday morning, our sisters Suad and Ilham arrived with their adult children. They came both because of Murida's declining health and to see me, but their arrival was not greatly welcomed. Murida's room was already filled with her own children and some of their spouses, and Murida didn't need her sisters and their children to further crowd her room.

In an attempt to bring a lighter spirit to the situation and to make her mother laugh, Mona whispered jokes about the interlopers, and Murida smiled. They both felt that the guests were coming to say goodbye, but Murida wouldn't hear of it. She felt it wasn't yet her time and wouldn't be for a long while.

Our mother and sister Inaam also arrived at Twam hospital on Saturday, as well as our aunt. I'd told them all that Murida was very ill and they should come. Two hours later, around one in the afternoon, the most anticipated visitor arrived from Beirut: our oldest sister, Muhiba. I'd been waiting for the moment when my two oldest sisters would meet, and I was very happy when I'd heard that Muhiba was coming. I knew that Murida wanted to see our oldest sister before she died. I didn't know if the reason was to make peace, but I hoped that was the case. I also hoped that stern Muhiba would soften her tough soul. Perhaps she would finally even accept Ghina.

In spite of my lack of faith, or maybe because of it, I believed strongly in the power of positive energy, especially when it was shared between people. Personally, I was more experienced in the power of negative energy, tortured as I was by polio, bad moods, and so many difficulties in the refugee camp. But I'd convinced myself that—just as negative energy could destroy—so positive energy could build. It *had* to be that way, I thought. If the sisters could exchange positive energy, then Murida would be in better shape to go to the other world. It didn't matter that I didn't believe in the afterlife. As long as my sister had faith, then I had to help her in her quest. I watched carefully as Muhiba entered the room. She was looking directly at her sister and at no one else.

"*Khayta*," Murida said, "you came. See what's happened to me?"

Muhiba interrupted Murida, kissing her sister's forehead and cheeks. Then she looked into her sister's face from less than a foot away. "Don't say that. You'll get better, and very soon God willing. You will go to your home, and we will visit you there, and you will be among your loved ones, and you'll see your grandchildren grow."

Muhiba was good with words, which had helped her become popular with neighbors and relatives. And she knew cancer: In twenty-two years, she hadn't forgiven the hated disease. Had he lived, Waleed would have been forty by then, married with lovely children, just like the rest of his siblings. Muhiba still thought that it was the work of an evil eye, of someone who'd envied her three beautiful boys.

Muhiba settled in and had a cordial conversation with me about my long trip and my family. She also greeted every one of her nieces, nephew, and sisters, as well as her mother and aunt, with the traditional kisses on the cheeks. Her daughter-in-law was no exception. At two o'clock, Amal's husband got carry-out food for everyone from a restaurant in downtown Al-Ain, which we ate in a nearby open area. Mahmoud kissed his mother and told her that he had to drive to Oman to renew his wife's passport. Mahmoud's wife was a Palestinian refugee like him, but had Omani citizenship, having grown up in Oman. It was less than a two-hour drive, and government offices would be open on Saturday.

Because Murida's room could not accommodate all the visitors, people moved in and out in groups. Those of us who weren't in the room paced the hallway. Since the previous night, Murida had been receiving more oxygen and morphine, and she was more restful, with her spells of sleepiness growing longer. Her breathing was also shallower, and her daughters felt good that their mother wasn't struggling as much. She must be better, many of them thought, including Mahmoud, who felt confident enough that he left his mother's side to get his wife's passport renewed. Maha knew otherwise and thought her mother "could go anytime." She and Amal had spent the previous night with their mother.

The only thing on my mind was for my sister to remain comfortable and to take her last breath in peace. Murida believed in heaven, and I believed in the power of faith. I put the two together and came to the conclusion that she should be at peace as she left this life. I believed that the state of mind she was in at the moment of her death would stay with her for the rest of time. I didn't want her to die while in pain, angry, scared, or resentful. This was the first time I'd realized that, although I didn't believe in a God, I was spiritual and respected the beliefs of others. Perhaps I had a faith, but didn't know it.

Around 4:30 p.m., while Ilham and I were in the room, I saw Murida's breaths decreasing in both frequency and length. They were becoming very shallow and short, and Murida's eyes had been closed for a few minutes. Murida stopped breathing—no, she just waited a very long time to take the next short breath. I wondered how many more breaths her lungs had left. I knew that her brain was nearly dead from hypoxia, and I wondered how long it would be before the rest of her followed and she left everyone else behind, each to their own feelings and memories. I felt it was time for people to say their goodbyes.

I went into the hallway and called for everyone to come and say goodbye to their mother, daughter, or sister, as she was taking her final breaths. As they all rushed in and looked at Murida's face, each had a different reaction. Murida's head was bent backwards onto the bedrail, she was pale, her mouth was slightly open. She looked peaceful—not smiling, not scared, and not tense. It must be the morphine, I thought.

A few cried silently, but most moaned and wailed. I asked them to be quiet, telling them that they didn't want her spirit to carry all that pain and grief, but no one listened. Suad yelled at me that this was the way that they grieved. I should've known that "one cried as loud and long as he had loved the deceased" and "one could not control one's feelings in such a moment." Ghina was crying quietly but with anger, Maha in silence, and Mona had tears streaking her face, but did not show signs of anguish. She must have a deep faith, I thought.

After a moment for tears, each daughter took turns kissing their mother's face and hand, and Mona kissed her mother's feet as well, a sign of utmost respect, love, and gratitude for what her mother had done for her. I thought later that I'd been selfish to ask people to change the emotional responses they'd learned over a lifetime. If I didn't want to risk Murida leaving with all that negative energy, then I should've waited until she took her last breath before calling them into the room. I finally reassured myself that Murida had taken one final very short breath as they'd all come in, and she almost surely didn't hear them.

When the moment was over, Murida's daughters noticed that their brother wasn't in the room with them. *Oh God*, each of them thought, *why did you have to take her at this moment? Her son didn't have a chance to say his goodbye.*

Of all his siblings, Mahmoud had been the quietest through his mother's illness. He had to be the strongest branch in his family's tree. He knew that, as the son, he had to appear strong for his mother's and sisters' sake. He was involved in every decision and was often the tie-breaker when sisters disagreed. He played the role of son and man of the house, and he relieved his father of having to participate in decision-making.

Under such a burden, Mahmoud had to defer experiencing his true feelings until after his mother died. Now that his mother was gone, he could feel sad, lonely, incomplete, and a stranger in a new world. Maybe he could even feel a little angry at fate for taking his mother prematurely. Who would he have become were Murida not his mother?

Our mother seemed upset at the loss of her daughter, but she was not as distraught as I'd expected. I'd expected her to wail, but instead she cried in silence and did not kiss her daughter. Our mother had been grieving since she'd laid eyes on Murida nearly a month before, and she must've run out of emotional energy.

Inaam was in a corner looking more distant than sad. I looked around, waiting particularly on Saleem's reaction. My brother-in-law mumbled a few words while giving a glance at Murida's body, and then left the room to call people on his cell phone, telling each the same thing: "The Hajji died." Ghina, like me, found it odd, coming from the man who'd wailed like a child when his wife was wheeled to have surgery seventeen months earlier. In the intervening months, he must have stopped counting on her recovery.

After the room cleared out a little, I sat by my sister's side, looked into her face, and tried to cry as I'd expected I would—but I couldn't. I scanned my mind for memories with my sister, but I couldn't force any emotion to the surface. I couldn't easily shed the role I'd been playing, the role of a doctor and decider of my sister's fate. It took me twenty-four hours before I faced my emotions and wept at my sister's grave like an abandoned child. Just as I'd been surprised at my lack of a strong emotional reaction while in the hospital, I was surprised at my childlike weeping in front of so many men. I had to be helped to a car and driven away.

As I left the room on that Saturday, Osama was stepping out of the elevator at the end of the hallway. Maha had called him in the morning and asked him to come, and he'd taken the bus from Abu Dhabi. When he was close to Murida's room, Maha said, "Teyta just died," and Osama suppressed a gasp. It was not good to cry aloud for lost loved one—or that's what he had learned from religion classes. Maha walked him to the room and lifted the white sheet from Murida's face. Once he saw his dear grandmother's face, he couldn't hold back his feelings any longer. He cried loudly while pressing his face to hers, just as the two had done when he was a baby.

At the hospital, Rafiq and I went downstairs in order to intercept Mahmoud and tell him that his mother's body was waiting for him. We wanted to get to him before others expressed their condolences, possibly confusing the final moment that he needed with his mother. Mona and I made sure no one else went into the room while Mahmoud was there. Mona stayed in the room and watched him, later telling me to make sure I wrote down how Mahmoud had sat down beside Murida, held her, and cried:

"Why did you leave me? I can't live without you. You made me, you made all of us. You helped us succeed, and now that it's time to repay you, you go away.

"Why did you leave my boys? Who will pray for their success? You won't be at their graduation. We'll never taste your food again. What will become of our home? What will happen to father? Who will understand him like you did? Who will care for him as you did?

"May God keep you in his heavens; I hope I am good enough to see you again."

EPILOGUE

The next day, Murida's daughters washed her body in accordance with Muslim tradition so that she could be buried.

Only blood relatives could see the body after death, and only men related by blood could place Murida's wrapped body in the grave. As was tradition, only men attended the burial—the women waited at home for the men to return.

Murida was laid to rest at Dubai's public burial grounds, and I had felt oddly sociable that day. I'd even laughed with a cousin who had been a childhood friend. I stood to the side as Mutasim and Mahmoud climbed down into the big hole and were handed

Murida's body wrapped in a white sheet. Osama helped carry her body down and gently handed it to them. My brothers were told how to place her body so that her head would be tilted slightly in the direction of Mecca.

It was the first time I'd ever witnessed a burial, as I'd missed my father's and Waleed's. I admired the emotional strength of both my older brother and my nephew, who performed their task with little instruction.

I was given a spot right next to the grave in order to be as close to the burial as my handicap allowed. If I'd been physically able, I could've been the one down in the hole burying my sister, an honor and duty I would never have because of my bout with polio. I wondered how I would've performed the task of carrying my sister's dead body. I might have clung to it and not released it, as I'd done when I visited my nephew Waleed's grave and fell on it, crying. Because I didn't believe in the afterlife, I had no spiritual feelings about the Muslim burial traditions, but I hated to see my sister gone: her life journey ending like this, her life over, buried under desert sand, away from the two countries where she'd been born and raised. Who would've guessed that Murida would end up buried in the Dubai desert? Surely her father would have wanted his strong daughter to be buried close to him, as he was buried next to his own mother.

As tradition required, close relatives of the deceased stood in a row by the grave and received the

men who came to pay their condolences. I stood between Muhiba's husband and my brother Mutasim.
Saleem, Mahmoud and Osama stood together next
to Mutasim. Slowly, as a long line of men passed and
shook everyone's hands—or sometimes kissed their
cheeks—I grew emotional.

The well of emotion filled up quickly, and, as a line
of teenagers and older children took their turn shaking hands, my emotions flooded over. These were my
grand-nephews, and I loved them like I'd loved their
parents before them. They were too young to lose a
young grandmother. What began as a realization of
loss turned into uncontrollable grief. As I wept for the
loss of my sister, I lost my strength to stand and was
helped to Ilham's husband's car. We left before the end
of the ritual. I could not understand how Mahmoud,
Osama, Mutasim, and Saleem were able to hold in
their feelings. Then I remembered that "men don't
cry"—that's what my aunt had told me when I wept
loudly over Waleed's grave twenty-two years earlier.

At Mona's house, women filled every room, some
weeping, others recalling Murida's great traits. A few
women roamed around, making sure everyone had
their needs fulfilled. They listened to tapes of the
Quran and waited for the men to return. The close
family members arrived first and went into the large
kitchen to eat. Shortly afterwards, the men left and the
women went into the kitchen to eat. Such was tradition.

Two weeks later, all six daughters—Hanan had come from Canada—went to their parents' house in order to go through and empty it. They decided that their father would take turns living with each of his children who lived in Sharjah.

As Murida's daughters went through the apartment, they were shocked to find so many unused bed sheets, towels, coffee cups, silverware, and clothes still in their plastic wrappers. She must have known that she had only a short time to live—they wondered why she didn't use some of them instead of keeping them all for the Beirut apartment. Everyone cried, and Amal sobbed as she said "she never had a chance to show these lovely things off in Beirut."

The spring after Murida's death, I was invited to give a medical presentation in Dubai. I spent a few days at Mona's, where I was visited daily by my nieces and other relatives. One evening, while everyone was present, Saleem got excited and shouted at no one in particular that, despite what people were claiming, he wasn't saying bad things about his son to some of his daughters.

At the peak of the farce, I heard Maha say to herself, "Dear Mother, God relieved you of having to deal with him any longer."

Two years after her mother's death, Mona immigrated to Canada with her family. She was followed, two years after that, by Mahmoud and his family. They wanted their children to become Canadian citizens and have a better life than they'd had as Palestinian refugees. A number of close relatives had already preceded them, making new lives in Toronto, including my youngest brother. Six years after they came to Canada, and all three children graduated, Mona and her kids went back to live with their father, who kept working in Dubai in order to send them money in Canada.

Our mother decided to stay in the Emirates. But Mutasim's life was disrupted by her presence, and she finally moved to an apartment near my sister Ilham and niece Saada.

My mother died five years after Murida, also in a November. She was also buried away from Palestine and Lebanon.

Six years after Murida's death, her children got together and rented their father his own apartment. He had spent the previous six years living with his son and daughters, mostly with Amal, who had a high tolerance for Saleem's erratic behavior.

Around the same time, Murida's firstborn grandson Osama got married. As at many other weddings, a professional photographer scanned old photos of the bride and groom, and these photos were projected onto a large screen. At one point, a photograph of

Osama and Murida appeared, and Osama choked and got teary-eyed. His mother saw him and started sobbing. All Maha's siblings at the wedding followed suit, including Mahmoud and Mona, who'd traveled from Canada to attend.

Every time a relative or family friend mentioned how much Murida would've enjoyed the wedding of her dearest grandchild, the family began to cry again.

"But her spirit is with us," Mona said. "She's looking down on us from heaven. She's happy for Osama, and she'd want us to be happy. So let's enjoy this moment the way she would've wanted." After that, they all enjoyed the rest of the wedding, with hearts full of love for their dear mother, Murida.

50272298R00140

Made in the USA
Charleston, SC
19 December 2015